LOW–FAT GOURMET
C H I C K E N

LOW–FAT GOURMET
CHICKEN
JACKIE EDDY & ELEANOR CLARK

KEY PORTER·BOOKS

Typography by Type & Graphics
Production by Carol Dondrea, Bookman Productions
Copyediting by Rosaleen Bertolino
Jacket design by The Dunlavey Studio

Canadian Cataloguing in Publication Data

Eddy, Jackie, 1931–
  Low-fat gourmet chicken

Canadian ed.
Includes index.
ISBN 1-55013-413-2

1. Low-fat diet—Recipes.   2. Low-cholesterol diet—Recipes.
3. Cookery (Chicken).   I. Clark, Eleanor, 1934–   .   II. Title.

RM237.7.E33   1992   641.6′65   C92-093095-6

Published by arrangement with Prima Publishing, Rocklin, CA

Published in Canada by:

Key Porter Books Limited
70 The Esplanade
Toronto, Ontario
M5E 1R2

Printed in the United States of America

92 93 94 95   5 4 3 2 1

Contents

Metric Equivalents

¼	teaspoon	=	1.25	milliliters
½	teaspoon	=	2.5	milliliters
1	teaspoon	=	5.0	milliliters
1½	teaspoons	=	7.5	milliliters
2	teaspoons	=	10.0	milliliters
1	tablespoon	=	15.0	milliliters
2	tablespoons	=	30.0	milliliters
¼	cup	=	62.5	milliliters
½	cup	=	125.0	milliliters
1	cup	=	250.0	milliliters
1½	cups	=	375.0	milliliters
2	cups	=	500.0	milliliters
¼	lb	=	125 grams	
½	lb	=	250 grams	
1	lb	=	500 grams	

200–205° Fahrenheit	=	95° Celsius
220–225° Fahrenheit	=	105° Celsius
245–250° Fahrenheit	=	120° Celsius
275° Fahrenheit	=	135° Celsius
300–305° Fahrenheit	=	150° Celsius
325–330° Fahrenheit	=	165° Celsius
345–350° Fahrenheit	=	175° Celsius
370–375° Fahrenheit	=	190° Celsius
400–405° Fahrenheit	=	205° Celsius
425–430° Fahrenheit	=	220° Celsius
445–450° Fahrenheit	=	230° Celsius
470–475° Fahrenheit	=	245° Celsius
500° Fahrenheit	=	260° Celsius

Introduction

With Information on Special
Low-Fat, Low-Salt Ingredients

This book offers chicken recipes that are low in fat and, in most cases, salt without sacrificing flavor, texture, and interest.

A recent issue of the *New England Journal of Medicine* featured a study that compared the fat content of three different cooked breasts of chicken: one with the skin attached, one that had the skin removed before cooking, and another that had the skin removed after cooking. The study showed that the chicken breasts all had the same amount of fat *after* removing the skin. So if you want to cook a chicken with the skin on, by all means do so, but remember that when you take the skin off, you take most of the flavor away as well. That's where *this* book comes in: We have over two hundred recipes for chicken, 98 percent of which cook chicken without the skin — each one a winner.

We've given helpful cooking tips at the beginning of most chapters in the book but, generally speaking, don't overcook breasts of chicken, particularly when they're boneless. Legs can take overcooking, but not those tender breasts. Inexperienced cooks tend to cook chicken at too high a heat. Use a gentler heat on chicken than you would for red meat or fish. High heat tends to harden the proteins in chicken, resulting in a tough end product. A word of caution though — chicken can be dangerous if undercooked, so do make sure it's cooked through, just not overcooked. Because chicken parts come in all shapes and sizes, cooking times will vary. Most of the chicken recipes tested in this book used birds weighing around 2½ to 3 pounds.

INGREDIENT INFORMATION

You must limit your total fat intake to no more than 30 percent of your total diet. You musn't eliminate fat completely from your diet, however. Your body does need some fat, but not *saturated fat* (animal fat and tropical oils such as palm, palm kernel, or coconut oils). The fats used in this book — safflower oil, canola oil, and olive oil — contain a high percentage of polyunsaturates or monounsaturates. Studies show that olive oil helps to lower cholesterol and blood pressure. It has a distinctive flavor and is a little heavier than the first two oils, making it more suitable for some dishes than others. We tested all of the recipes calling for soft margarine with Becel, a nonhydrogenated margarine composed of approximately 40 percent polyunsaturates, 40 percent monounsaturates, and 20 percent saturated fats. In the recipes calling for margarine, be sure you choose a margarine with the highest percentage of polyunsaturated fat and the lowest percentage of saturated fat that you can find. Don't buy margarine that uses *hydrogenated* oil — it's as bad as cholesterol.

If you are on a salt-reduced diet as well as a low-fat one, whenever we call for chicken stock or bouillon, use your homemade stock or choose a low-sodium commercial one. The nutritional analyses are based on the use of canned unsalted broth since it is impossible to analyze homemade broths. The honey we used for testing was Bee Maid brand honey.

You'll notice that the following ingredients appear in the recipes again and again: no-salt seasoning, lemon pepper, and no-stick vegetable oil spray. No-salt seasoning adds "zip" to low-salt recipes. Commercial brands are available in most supermarkets but we prefer to make our own (see the recipe in Chapter 10). Lemon pepper is a popular seasoning, but be aware that many brands have that four-letter word *salt* as their main ingredient. Check the label carefully; low-salt and no-salt brands are available. An increasing number of no-stick vegetable oil sprays are on the market. Be sure to choose one without cholesterol, or make your own by pouring safflower or canola oil into a glass or plastic spray bottle.

Dijon mustard is delicious, and high in salt. If you're on a salt-restricted diet, you'll probably want to avoid the recipes containing mustard. As this book went to press, however, we discovered that no-salt and low-salt Dijon mustards can sometimes be found in health food stores. Give them a try!

Just about all of the ingredients in this book are commonly available in supermarkets. You'll find some of the more exotic, such as sesame oil, hoisin sauce, and rice vinegar, in the imported foods section.

Finally, it's *most* important that you remember to include exercise in your new low-fat lifestyle. Exercise is very important in helping to lower your cholesterol level.

Good luck with our book . . . and good luck with your life!

1

Soups

Chicken is ideally suited to producing good stock. It has a good flavor and, if enough bones are used, it creates the gelatin so important to a full-bodied stock. The sturdy older birds have a better flavor for soup than the younger ones. Don't ever discard the necks, backs, and wings that you don't use, for they have a much greater bone to meat ratio and are ideal for the stockpot. Tuck them in the freezer until you have enough for stock (about 3 pounds).

HINTS ON SOUP MAKING

- Simmer soups rather than boiling them — the vegetables and meat will be more tender.
- The smaller the pieces of vegetables and meat, the faster the soup will cook.
- Soups keep for 4 to 5 days maximum in the refrigerator, but they freeze well – keeping up to 5 months.
- Always save leftover vegetable water. Drain and cool in the refrigerator. If you're not going to be using it within 2 to 3 days, store it in the freezer.
- Seasonings and herbs often become stronger when soup is reheated, so be aware of this when you add them to the soup the first time around.
- Onions are a *must* in every soup pot. Carrots and celery rank second in importance. You can use garlic freely, but for a mellower flavor, it's best not to peel it. And don't forget parsley — a welcome addition.
- Just about any herb can be used in soups, but be cautious with spices. Peppercorns are the exception — they are a must — but other than the occasional clove (stick one or two in an onion), or pinch of nutmeg, nothing else seems to work as well, in our experience.

3

Chicken Stock*

We're giving more than one recipe for chicken stock, as this is something that's called for throughout the book. Canned chicken broth is fine but has a very high salt content, so it's best to make your own whenever possible. The terms stock *and* broth *are interchangeable, although, technically,* stock *is made from bones and broth is made from meat. Most of our stock recipes use both bones and meat. Bouillon is the French term for stock or broth. (So if we call for bouillon, you know we're just being fancy!) You might find it useful to freeze stock in ice cube trays. Transfer to freezer bags and use when needed. The cooked chicken meat can be used for salads or casseroles.*

Stock 1

1	package chicken parts (2½ pounds)
¼	inch slice fresh ginger root
2	teaspoons no-salt seasoning (or salt substitute)**
2	green onions, chopped

In a large pot, place the chicken pieces and cover with water (about 6 cups). Add the ginger, no-salt seasoning, and onions. Bring to a boil. Reduce heat and simmer, uncovered, for 1½ hours, skimming off the foam that rises to the surface. Remove from heat and let cool. Remove the chicken and strain the stock. Refrigerate or freeze. Will keep in the refrigerator for 4 days and in the freezer for 4 to 5 months. Before using, remove the fat layer from the surface.

Makes 6 cups.

*Because homemade chicken stock is impossible to analyze nutritionally, there are no data available for it.

**You can use salt instead of salt substitute in your homemade stock and it will still be far less salty than the commercial brands. See also the recipe for No-Salt Seasoning on page 263.

Stock 2

Save all of the bones from boned chicken breasts and parts you don't use such as necks, backs, and wings. You can keep these in the freezer until you have enough to make some stock. You'll need at least 3 pounds. Use the same recipe as Stock 1 but increase the ginger to 2 slices.

Makes 6 cups.

Stock 3 with Cooked Carcass

This is a good stock to make with a large leftover roasting chicken or turkey, or you can use a 4-pound boiling chicken.

1   large chicken or turkey carcass
6   cups cold water
1   cup celery, chopped (include some leaves)
     Few sprigs parsley
1   large onion, sliced
1   large carrot, sliced
2   teaspoons salt substitute (or 1 teaspoon salt plus 1 teaspoon
        salt substitute)
3   peppercorns
1   bay leaf
1   teaspoon poultry seasoning

Place the carcass in a large soup pot and add all of the above ingredients. Bring to a boil. Reduce heat and simmer, covered, for 3 hours. Remove the bones, strain the broth, and cool. Refrigerate or freeze. Store in a covered container in the refrigerator no longer than 4 days or in the freezer for up to 4 to 5 months. Remove surface fat before using.

Makes 6 cups.

Stock 4 (Microwave)

3   pounds chicken parts (can be backs, necks, and wings)
1   leek, sliced
1   onion, sliced
1   stalk celery, sliced (include some leaves)
1   carrot, sliced
¼   cup fresh parsley, chopped
2   bay leaves
2   cloves
2   teaspoons poultry seasoning
4   black peppercorns
1   teaspoon salt substitute (or salt)
5   cups water

Combine all of the above ingredients in a large casserole. Cover with wax paper and cook on high for 15 to 20 minutes or until boiling. Turn the chicken parts over and stir. Cover and cook on medium for 1 hour. Let stand covered for 10 minutes. Strain and refrigerate or freeze. Remove fat before using.

Makes 5 cups.

Chicken Broccoli Soup

Try this nourishing supper dish. Some home baked biscuits or rolls would be a welcome addition. With such a fat-free meal you can splurge with dessert.

Serves 4.

1	half chicken breast, on the bone but with skin removed
2	cups water
12	ounces broccoli, chopped
1	stalk celery, chopped
1	small to medium onion, chopped
1	medium potato, peeled and diced
1	tablespoon lemon juice
3	cloves garlic, chopped
1	teaspoon no-salt seasoning
½	teaspoon paprika
	Dash of nutmeg
	Dash of white pepper
1	small can (7 oz.) low-fat evaporated milk

Place the chicken breast in a soup pot with the cold water. Bring to a boil. Immediately reduce heat and simmer until tender (about 12 to 15 minutes). Remove the chicken. After the chicken cools, remove the meat from the bones and dice. Meanwhile, skim any foam off the top of the stock and add all of the remaining ingredients (except the evaporated milk and chicken) to the pot. Cover and heat to boiling; reduce heat and simmer until vegetables are tender, about 15 minutes. Do not drain. Pour this mixture into a blender or food processor and blend until of uniform consistency — about 45 seconds. Return to the pot and add the evaporated milk and the diced chicken. Heat to just boiling. Garnish with a slice of fresh lemon if desired.

Each serving provides:			
140	Calories	18 g	Carbohydrate
14 g	Protein	112 mg	Sodium
2 g	Fat	26 mg	Cholesterol

Chicken Bouillon with Cubetti

We've given several recipes for chicken stock, which is used in many recipes throughout the book, but the same stock can become a knockout soup course at an elegant dinner party. (Of course, now we have to call it "bouillon.") When you serve it as a soup, you may want to add cubetti. A few comments on the ingredients in cubetti: First, note that the recipe calls for an egg. While we are still advised to limit eggs, the amount of cholesterol we get from the few cubetti in the soup will be negligible. Second, Parmesan cheese has a high fat content, but the small amount you will be consuming in the cubetti is not significant.

This soup is really quite special, but if you are concerned about fat, you could serve the following Chicken Bouillon with Vushka and still impress your guests.

Serves 8.

2-2½ quarts hot chicken stock

Cubetti:

½	pound ricotta (part skim milk) cheese (at room temperature)
1	large egg
1	egg yolk
1	teaspoon salt or salt substitute
	Pinch of nutmeg
¾	cup freshly grated Parmesan cheese

Beat the ricotta with an electric mixer until smooth. Add the egg, egg yolk, salt (or salt substitute), nutmeg, and Parmesan cheese. Blend well with a rubber spatula and spread in a greased 8-inch square glass baking dish. Place this dish in a larger, shallow baking pan filled with 1 inch of hot water and bake in a preheated 300° oven for about 45 minutes, or until firm. Cool completely, then cut into very small cubes (about ¼-inch square). The cubetti may be prepared two to three days before serving, but bring the cubes to room temperature before using.

Fill soup bowls or rimmed soup plates with hot chicken stock and add about 6 cubetti to each serving. A little minced fresh parsley sprinkled on top is nice as a garnish.

Each serving provides:			
132	Calories	4 g	Carbohydrate
11 g	Protein	550 mg	Sodium
8 g	Fat	69 mg	Cholesterol

Chicken Bouillon with Vushka

Serves 5.

5   cups hot chicken stock

Vushka

2   teaspoons finely chopped onion
½   cup finely chopped mushrooms
1   clove garlic, finely minced
1   tablespoon soft margarine
       Salt substitute and pepper to taste
½   teaspoon flour
10   wonton wrappers*

Sauté the onion, mushrooms, and garlic in soft margarine until onions are soft. Add salt, pepper, and flour. Cool. Place 1 teaspoon of filling on each wonton wrapper. Fold the wrapper over to form a triangle. Seal the edges with a flour and water paste. (Mix 1 teaspoon flour with 1½ teaspoons water.) Makes approximately 6 to 8 Vushka. Allow at least 2 triangles per person.

Cook the Vushka in simmering chicken stock for 5 minutes. Serve hot.

*The remaining wonton skins may be tightly wrapped and frozen for future use.

Each serving provides:

90	Calories	9 g	Carbohydrate
4 g	Protein	88 mg	Sodium
4 g	Fat	0 mg	Cholesterol

Slimmer's Chicken Cabbage Soup

As food writers, we find that this particular soup is probably our most requested recipe every year just after the holidays. Yes, January is the time to "pay the piper" for all of December's excesses. A bowl of this soup in place of lunch or dinner is guaranteed to show results on the bathroom scale. The soup is only 22 calories per serving so feel free to have a bowl at anytime, day or night, when those old hunger pangs strike.

Serves 5.

2	cups chicken stock
1	cup onion, finely chopped
1	medium tomato, chopped
½	green pepper, minced
½	teaspoon salt
¼	teaspoon freshly ground black pepper
1	teaspoon caraway seeds
2	teaspoons white wine vinegar
3	cups cold water
3	cups shredded cabbage
1	packet (¼ teaspoon) of Sugar Twin (or comparable sugar substitute)

Place the first seven ingredients in a soup pot and simmer for 20 minutes. Add the vinegar, water, cabbage, and Sugar Twin, bring to a boil, then simmer until the cabbage is soft (10 to 12 minutes).

Each serving provides:

43	Calories	7 g	Carbohydrate
2 g	Protein	251 mg	Sodium
1 g	Fat	0 mg	Cholesterol

Easy Leftover Chicken Soup

Serves 6.

1	tablespoon soft margarine
1	medium onion, chopped
1	medium carrot, chopped
1	stalk celery, chopped
2	cups cooked chicken, chopped
2½	cups homemade chicken stock, or 2 cans (10 oz. each) commercial broth
2½	cups water*

Melt the margarine in a large saucepan over medium heat. Sauté the onion, carrot, and celery for 2 to 3 minutes until the onion is softened. Stir in the chicken, stock, and water. Bring to a boil over high heat. Reduce heat to low, cover, and simmer for 10 to 12 minutes or until vegetables are tender.

This is the bare-bones recipe, but you can add to it in many ways. Bake a potato, cook up one or two other vegetables of your choice (such as broccoli, peas, spinach, acorn squash, fennel, even sweet potato). Puree the cooked vegetables in a food processor and add to the soup. This doesn't add many calories but does add lots of nutrition, and that's what we should be striving for, right? You can also enrich the soup with a little olive oil, soft margarine, or grated lowfat cheese if you want to change its character a bit.

*If you're using homemade stock, substitute an additional 2½ cups of the stock for the water.

Each serving provides:

146	Calories	3 g	Carbohydrate
18 g	Protein	668 mg	Sodium
6 g	Fat	42 mg	Cholesterol

Chicken Lentil Soup

Easy to make and even easier to eat! As with any homemade soup, it's smart to make a big pot and freeze the extra in serving sizes to have on hand whenever you want a good bowl of soup.

Serves 8 to 10.

4	chicken legs, skin and all visible fat removed
7	cups cold water
2	cups lentils, picked over and rinsed
4	ribs celery, chopped
4	carrots, chopped
1	onion, chopped
1	large can (28 oz.) tomatoes, chopped
2	cloves garlic, minced
½	cup minced fresh parsley
1½	teaspoons no-salt seasoning
¼	teaspoon freshly ground black pepper
2	cups chicken broth
2	tablespoons wine vinegar (optional)
	Pinch oregano (optional)

Place all of the ingredients (except the chicken broth, vinegar, and oregano) in a large soup pot or Dutch oven. Simmer, covered, for 1½ hours. Skim the froth off the top as needed. Add the chicken broth during the last 15 minutes of cooking. Taste before serving. If you think it needs a little more "zip," add the vinegar and oregano. Some people, however, like this soup best without these last two additions.

Each serving provides:

261	Calories	34 g	Carbohydrate
26 g	Protein	238 mg	Sodium
3 g	Fat	46 mg	Cholesterol

Chicken Minestrone

Good "stick-to-your-ribs" soup that can be a whole meal. Main-course soups are not only economical and nutritious but also practical. They can be prepared in advance and when reheated taste as good as new . . . sometimes even better!

Serves 8 to 10.

1	whole chicken breast, on the bone, skin removed
6	cups water
2	carrots, sliced
2	celery stalks, sliced
1	onion, chopped
4	cloves garlic, chopped
½	cup dried green split peas
1	large can (28 oz.) tomatoes
½	teaspoon oregano
½	teaspoon basil
¼	teaspoon rosemary
¼	teaspoon thyme
2	teaspoons no-salt seasoning
1½	cups broken spaghetti, uncooked

Place the chicken in a Dutch oven, add water, and bring to a boil. Reduce heat and simmer for 12 minutes. Remove the chicken and set aside. Skim the foam from the top of the liquid and add all remaining ingredients except the spaghetti. (Before adding the tomatoes, drain the juice into the Dutch oven and puree the tomatoes in a blender or food processor.) Simmer for 1½ hours. Add the broken spaghetti and simmer for an additional 8 minutes. Strip the chicken meat from the bone, dice, and add to the pot. Simmer for 2 minutes, and serve.

This soup freezes very well. Freeze in serving sizes and have a handy, nourishing lunch or supper on hand when you don't feel like cooking.

Each serving provides:

169	Calories	28 g	Carbohydrate
12 g	Protein	178 mg	Sodium
1 g	Fat	15 mg	Cholesterol

Lo-Cal Chinese Soup

This recipe came to us from a fellow food writer, who used this soup as part of a very successful weight reduction program. The original recipe called for the addition of 12 fresh or frozen shrimp. However, experts believe shrimp consumption should be limited. You would definitely miss it in a shrimp cocktail, but not in this soup. The bamboo shoots, straw mushrooms, baby corn, and rice noodles are available in the imported foods section of many supermarkets.

Serves 3 to 4.

2	cups chicken stock (preferably homemade)
1	teaspoon shredded fresh ginger
1	clove garlic, minced
½	cup fresh snow peas
¼	cup canned bamboo shoots, diced
¼	cup canned straw mushrooms
¼	cup canned baby corn (each corn cut in half)
1	whole chicken breast, boned, skinned, and diced
2	tablespoons fresh cilantro
	Handful of Chinese rice noodles
	Salt and pepper to taste

Add all ingredients to a soup pot and simmer gently until the chicken is cooked (approximately 15 to 20 minutes).

Each serving provides:

201	Calories	27 g	Carbohydrate
17 g	Protein	91 mg	Sodium
2 g	Fat	34 mg	Cholesterol

Phil's "South of the Border" Chicken Soup

Two bowls of this spicy soup are guaranteed to prevent a cough or cold for two months (according to Phil)!

Serves 4 to 6.

2½-3 pounds chicken parts, skin and all visible fat removed
2   cups canned tomatoes
1   large clove garlic, minced
½   cup green onion, chopped
⅔   cup canned green chilies, seeded and diced*
2   cups cooked garbanzo beans

Place the chicken in a Dutch oven or large saucepan. Add enough water to cover. Simmer about 30 minutes or until tender. Remove the chicken from the pot and add the tomatoes, garlic, onion, and chilies. Carefully take the meat from the bones and return the meat to the broth. Add the garbanzo beans and simmer for an additional 15 minutes. Serve with warm flour tortillas. To warm tortillas, wrap in a damp towel and place in a warm (200°) oven for about 20 minutes.

*If you prefer a milder tasting soup, reduce the chilies to ⅓ cup.

Each serving provides:			
252	Calories	24 g	Carbohydrate
28 g	Protein	348 mg	Sodium
5 g	Fat	69 mg	Cholesterol

2

Salads and Other Hot Weather Dishes

Salads are not only nutritious and delectable, but also one of today's most versatile dishes, as you'll see in these next few pages.

You'll find some delicious salads in this chapter. We've added tender-crisp (cooked until tender but still crisp) vegetables to some and interesting fruits to others. You'll discover some popular pasta salads as well as savory rice and tasty molded salads. We've also included some chilled chicken entrées that are perfect for hot weather. It's a good idea to have a poached chicken breast or two on hand (see Best Ever Method for Cooking Chicken Breasts, this chapter) and ready for slicing into salads, sandwiches, and quick casseroles, particularly in the summer.

HINTS FOR GREAT SALADS

Molded Salads

- When making a *large* molded salad, use ¼ cup less liquid than the recipe calls for to guarantee that it congeals properly. Minimum time for gelatin to set well is usually 6 hours.
- Always use canned pineapple for molded salads calling for pineapple — if you use fresh, the gelatin won't gel.
- To improvise a ring mold, place a greased can in the center of a well-greased casserole dish.
- For patio entertaining serve individual gelatin molds in paper cups.

Green Salads

- For crisp salad greens, wash well in cool water. Drain well and wrap in a cloth dish towel or paper towels. Put towel-wrapped greens in the refrigerator for several hours.
- When trying to determine the amount of lettuce needed for a large tossed green salad, a good rule of thumb is 3 quarts of torn-up lettuce for 10 to 12 people.

- To keep head lettuce fresh, wash the head under cold water, drain, and wrap in paper towels that have been moistened with cold water. Store in the refrigerator.
- Dressing shouldn't be added to the salad until the last minute; the oil causes lettuce to wilt.

Finally, some good advice from Jackie's mother: "If you can't make a good fruit salad, don't." Fruit salad is only as good as the quality of the fruit you use. You simply can't hide overripe or underripe fruit in a salad. Keep this in mind should you decide to serve a fruit salad with some cold sliced chicken — lovely for a special brunch or lunch. For a very simple fruit salad, stir about 3 tablespoons frozen orange juice concentrate (thawed) over cut-up fresh fruit. We like to start with a can of drained pineapple chunks and then add the freshest and sweetest fruit we can find, including diced peaches, pears, melon, kiwi, and a handful of fresh or frozen blueberries. Any combination of the freshest fruit available would be suitable.

Best Ever Method for Cooking Chicken Breasts

The very best way to cook chicken for a salad or for plain sliced cold chicken is the following "steamed" method. The Chinese have been doing this for centuries. The chicken is actually steeped rather than cooked, resulting in moist white chicken pieces.

Whole chicken breasts, with bone and skin left on (as many as you want to cook)
2   green onions, chopped

Place the chicken breasts in a large pot, just big enough to hold them. Add enough water to cover the chicken plus ½ inch over. Remove the chicken. Add the green onions to the water and bring to a boil. Lower the chicken carefully back into the pot. When water returns to a boil, boil for 3 *minutes*. Cover tightly and turn heat *off*. Let the chicken sit for a minimum of 3 hours. It can sit for as long as 6 hours, but should be refrigerated after 4 hours of sitting. Do *not* lift the lid during this time.

Remove the chicken from the pot and strain the stock. Refrigerate. When the fat congeals on top, remove and freeze the stock to use in soups and sauces. It's most convenient for later use to freeze the stock in small (1- or 2-cup) containers.

Each half breast provides:			
108	Calories	0 g	Carbohydrate
21 g	Protein	45 mg	Sodium
2 g	Fat	55 mg	Cholesterol

Almond Chicken Salad

This is a wonderful summertime lunch or supper dish. Everyone loves this salad. Some nice yeasty rolls, white or whole wheat, or a mixture of both, would be all you need to complete the meal. Almond oil is polyunsaturated, making it one of the most healthful nuts.

Serves 8.

3	whole chicken breasts, cooked, skinned, and coarsely cubed*
1	can (10 oz.) water chestnuts, drained and sliced
1½	cups red or green seedless grapes
1	cup sliced celery
1	to 1½ cups toasted, slivered almonds
1	can (10 to 14 oz.) pineapple chunks, drained
1	can (10 oz.) mandarin oranges, drained

Place all of the above ingredients into a large bowl and toss with the following dressing.

Dressing

1	cup soft tofu, drained
¼	cup low-fat yogurt
1½	teaspoons sugar
2¼	teaspoons curry powder
2¼	teaspoons low-sodium soy sauce
½	teaspoon ginger
½	teaspoon lemon pepper
1½	teaspoons red wine vinegar

Blend all of the dressing ingredients in a blender or food processor and toss with the salad.

*See Best Ever Method for Cooking Chicken Breasts in this chapter.

Each serving provides:			
335	Calories	27 g	Carbohydrate
27 g	Protein	223 mg	Sodium
14 g	Fat	55 mg	Cholesterol

Chinese Chicken Salad

The rice vinegar and sesame oil are available in the imported foods section of many supermarkets.

Serves 4 to 6.

3   cups lettuce torn into bite-size pieces
1½   cups cooked chicken, diced
1   can (8 oz.) water chestnuts, drained and sliced
½   cup carrots, julienned
½   cup green onions, sliced diagonally
½   of a red cabbage, shredded
1   small can (6 oz.) chow mein noodles

In a large bowl, combine all salad ingredients except the noodles. Just before serving, toss the salad ingredients with the dressing and decorate the top with the noodles.

Note: Frozen snow peas (defrosted and patted dry) or bamboo shoots make great additions.

Dressing

3   tablespoons low-sodium soy sauce
1   tablespoon canola oil
2   tablespoons rice vinegar
1   tablespoon sugar
1   teaspoon garlic powder
½   teaspoon sesame oil
½   teaspoon black pepper

Combine the dressing ingredients and whisk together until smooth. Set aside.

Each serving provides:			
360	Calories	36 g	Carbohydrate
18 g	Protein	565 mg	Sodium
17 g	Fat*	37 mg	Cholesterol

*Although this is mostly the "good" type of fat, you may want to save this recipe for a special occasion.

Oriental Chicken Salad

Makes a nice low-calorie lunch. The rice vinegar, sesame oil, and hoisin sauce are available in the imported foods section of most supermarkets.

Serves 4 to 6.

3½	cups cooked chicken, diced
1	cup snow peas, blanched and chilled
1	small can (10 oz.) water chestnuts, drained and diced
3	medium carrots, shaved with vegetable peeler
¾	cup green pepper, chopped

Mix all salad ingredients together in a bowl.

Dressing

1	tablespoon plus 1 teaspoon canola or safflower oil
4	tablespoons rice vinegar
1	tablespoon plus 1 teaspoon sesame oil
1	tablespoon low-sodium soy sauce
1	tablespoon lemon juice
1	tablespoon hoisin sauce

Shake all dressing ingredients together in a jar and pour over the salad. Toss lightly and chill. Toss lightly again just before serving.

Each serving provides:			
322	Calories	16 g	Carbohydrate
30 g	Protein	414 mg	Sodium
15 g	Fat*	87 mg	Cholesterol

*Although this is mostly the "good" type of fat, you may want to save this recipe for a special occasion.

Chicken and Snow Pea Salad

The crunch of snow peas and broccoli infused with a sesame-flavored dressing make this salad extremely popular. Leftovers can be stuffed into pita bread for lunch the following day. Great picnic fare as well.

Serves 4.

2	cups fresh snow peas, lightly steamed, then chilled
1	cup diced carrots, lightly steamed, then chilled
1	whole chicken breast, cooked, skinned, and cut into strips
¼	pound fresh bean sprouts
1	cup raw broccoli flowerets
6	fresh mushrooms, brushed clean or peeled and sliced
1	small head romaine lettuce, washed and torn into bite-size pieces

Don't oversteam the pea pods or carrots. They must be tender but crisp. Steam the snow peas and carrots separately; steam the snow peas for 1 minute and the carrots for 2 minutes. They should be chilled immediately under cold running water to stop the cooking process. Pat dry or wrap in paper towels to remove excess moisture.

Toss all of the above ingredients in a large salad bowl with the following dressing. Try serving this salad with chopsticks for fun.

Oriental Dressing

⅓	cup safflower or canola oil
2	tablespoons sesame oil (found in imported foods section of supermarket)
2	tablespoons apple cider vinegar
1	teaspoon brown sugar
1	teaspoon fresh ginger, finely grated
1	tablespoon low-sodium soy sauce
⅓	teaspoon garlic powder

Place dressing ingredients in a jar and shake well.

Each serving provides:

384	Calories	18 g	Carbohydrate
20 g	Protein	214 mg	Sodium
27 g	Fat*	37 mg	Cholesterol

---

*Although this is mostly the "good" type of fat, you may want to save this recipe for a special occasion.

Chicken Salad with Honey Poppyseed Dressing

This is a dynamite salad. If you are serving a simple (sauceless) chicken entrée, omit the diced chicken from this salad and you have the perfect accompaniment. Avocados are high in fat, but it's the "good" type. Avocados contain 11 vitamins and 17 minerals, and are low in sodium and high in potassium. So go for it!

Serves 4 to 5.

1	head romaine lettuce
1	small whole chicken breast, cooked, skinned, and diced
1	can (10 oz.) Mandarin oranges, drained
½	red onion, thinly sliced
1	banana, diced
1	avocado, peeled and diced

Wash the lettuce, drain well, and wrap in paper towels or a tea towel to remove excess moisture. Tear into bite-size pieces and place in a salad bowl. Add the remaining salad ingredients and toss with the following dressing when ready to serve.

Honey Poppyseed Dressing

⅓	cup honey
½	cup canola or safflower oil
1	teaspoon grated onion
3	tablespoons white wine vinegar
2	tablespoons lemon juice
½	teaspoon dry mustard
½	teaspoon no-salt seasoning
1	teaspoon poppyseeds

Heat the honey for a few seconds in the microwave (it will blend better with the oil) and combine all of the dressing ingredients in a jar and shake well. If you don't have a microwave available to heat the honey, combine all of the ingredients (except the poppyseeds) in a blender. Add the poppyseeds after the dressing is blended.

Each serving provides:			
560	Calories	50 g	Carbohydrate
15 g	Protein	53 mg	Sodium
36 g	Fat*	26 mg	Cholesterol

*Although this is mostly the "good" type of fat, you may want to save this recipe for a special occasion.

Chicken Salad with Honey Yogurt Dressing

Nice light summertime fare.

Serves 6.

2-3   cups cooked chicken breast, cut into bite-size strips
1   large or 2 small unpeeled apples, diced
2   cups celery, diced
1   large red pepper, diced and seeded
2   cups fresh mushrooms, sliced

Dressing

1   cup low-fat yogurt
1   tablespoon fresh lemon juice
¼   cup honey
1½   teaspoons grated orange peel

Place the chicken, apples and vegetables in a salad bowl. Combine the dressing ingredients and toss with the salad.

Each serving provides:			
199	Calories	22 g	Carbohydrate
21 g	Protein	108 mg	Sodium
3 g	Fat	52 mg	Cholesterol

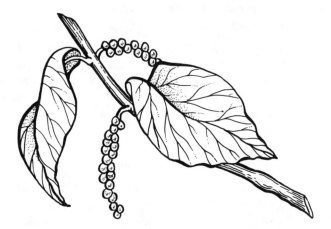

Mexican Salad

Serves 6 as a main course for lunch,
but will serve 10 to 12 as a buffet side-dish.

1	head iceberg lettuce, shredded
½	of a small red cabbage, finely shredded
1	small to medium red onion, very thinly sliced
1	can (14 oz.) kidney beans, well drained
2	cups low-fat mozzarella cheese, shredded
3	cups cooked chicken breast, diced

Put half of the lettuce in the bottom of a large salad bowl. Top with the red cabbage, then the red onion. Layer the kidney beans over the onion, the cheese over the kidney beans, then the chicken over the cheese, and top with the remaining lettuce. This can be assembled a few hours before serving and stored in the re-frigerator. Just before serving, toss with the following dressing.

Dressing

½	cup safflower oil
½	cup lemon juice
¾	teaspoon cumin
¾	teaspoon lemon pepper*
⅛	teaspoon black pepper
1¾	tablespoons sugar
2½	teaspoons chili powder

Put all dressing ingredients in a jar and shake well. Pour over salad and toss.

*Club House brand lemon pepper is low in salt; other salt-free and low-salt brands are also available. (Check the label.)

Each serving provides:			
485	Calories	23 g	Carbohydrate
37 g	Protein	444 mg	Sodium
28 g	Fat*	82 mg	Cholesterol

*Although this is mostly the "good" type of fat, you may want to save this recipe for a special occasion.

Pasta Bow Chicken Salad

Serves 6.

2   cups uncooked pasta bows
2   cups cooked chicken, cut into bite-size pieces
1   can (10 oz.) mandarin oranges, drained
½   cup pitted black olives, sliced
1   small red onion, thinly sliced
¼   cup toasted slivered almonds

Cook the pasta bows according to the package instructions. Drain and rinse in cold water. Turn into a bowl and add the chicken, oranges, olives, and onion. Chill at least 1 hour. When ready to serve, pour the dressing over the salad and toss. Garnish with the almonds.

Dressing

⅓   cup lime juice
3   tablespoons canola oil or safflower oil
¼   cup honey
1½   tablespoons fresh ginger, peeled and grated
1½   teaspoons grated lime peel
      No-salt seasoning and pepper to taste

Mix all dressing ingredients together. This dressing is best made 1 to 2 hours ahead of time to allow the flavors to blend.

Each serving provides:

403	Calories	49 g	Carbohydrate
20 g	Protein	147 mg	Sodium
15 g	Fat	42 mg	Cholesterol

Doreen's Pasta Salad

You can also make this without the chicken for a super accompaniment to barbecued poultry.

Serves 4 to 6.

3	cups uncooked fusilli (spiral-shaped) pasta
⅓	cup safflower or canola oil
	Juice of ½ lemon
½	teaspoon oregano leaves
1	clove garlic, minced
1	sweet red pepper, chopped
1	green pepper, chopped
1	medium cucumber, peeled, seeded, and chopped
½	cup radishes, sliced
½	cup black olives, sliced
8	green onions, sliced
1	cup cooked chicken, cubed

Gradually add the fusilli to rapidly boiling salted water, so that the water continues to boil. Cook uncovered, stirring occasionally, until tender but firm (*al dente*). Rinse under cold running water and drain again. Place in a large bowl.

Combine the oil, lemon juice, oregano, and garlic in a jar. Shake well and pour over the fusilli. Add the remaining ingredients. Toss to coat well and let chill for at least 2 hours for the flavors to blend before serving.

Each serving provides:			
406	Calories	44 g	Carbohydrate
16 g	Protein	153 mg	Sodium
19 g	Fat*	25 mg	Cholesterol

*Although this is mostly the "good" type of fat, you may want to save this recipe for a special occasion.

Chicken Pasta Salad with Creamy Dressing

A great main dish for a warm summer night. Minus the chicken, it would be a great accompaniment to grilled salmon steaks.

Serves 4 to 6.

2	cups uncooked macaroni (plain or whole wheat or a mixture of both)
½	cup frozen peas, thawed
1	cup cooked chicken, cubed
¼	cup green onion, sliced
½	cup celery, diced
⅔	cup fresh mushrooms, sliced (don't use canned)
1	small jar (2 oz.) chopped pimientos, drained

To cook the macaroni, bring 2 quarts of water to a boil. Stir in the macaroni and cook until done (about 7 to 10 minutes). Drain the macaroni and rinse with cold water to cool. Drain well. Add the peas, chicken, green onion, celery, mushrooms, and pimientos. Mix well, then stir in the following dressing. (It might look as though there's too much dressing, but the macaroni will soak it up.) Refrigerate until serving time. Spoon into a large bowl, lined with lettuce, or into large lettuce cups on individual plates.

Creamy Dressing

1	cup reduced-calorie mayonnaise
½	cup buttermilk
¼	cup sugar

Mix the dressing ingredients well and stir into the macaroni mixture. This should be made at least four hours in advance of serving.

Each serving provides:

407	Calories	49 g	Carbohydrate
16 g	Protein	342 mg	Sodium
16 g	Fat*	42 mg	Cholesterol

---

*Although this is mostly the "good" type of fat, you may want to save this recipe for a special occasion.

Overnight Curried Rice Salad

This looks quite spectacular at a buffet. The brightly colored diced peppers and the dark currants make a wonderful contrast to the curry-colored rice.

Serves 10 to 12.

2	whole cooked chicken breasts
8	cups cooked long grain rice
1	cup (each) red, green, and yellow bell peppers, finely diced
1	cup green onion, sliced
1	cup black currants
⅓	cup fresh parsley, finely minced

Dressing

¼	cup olive oil
¼	cup white wine vinegar
¼	cup apple juice concentrate
¼	cup fresh lemon juice
2	tablespoons plus 1 teaspoon curry powder
½	teaspoon black pepper
1	teaspoon no-salt seasoning
2	tablespoons light corn syrup

Remove the skin and bones from the chicken breasts and dice. Place the chicken, rice, peppers, green onion, currants, and parsley in a large bowl. Put the dressing ingredients in a jar and shake well. Pour over the salad and toss together to combine. Cover the salad and chill for at least 12 hours to allow the flavors to blend. Toss again before serving.

Each serving provides:			
363	Calories	60 g	Carbohydrate
15 g	Protein	37 mg	Sodium
7 g	Fat	27 mg	Cholesterol

Chicken and Wild Rice Salad McCaffery

This is a huge hit at brunches and lunches!

Serves 8.

1	cup wild rice (cooked according to directions below)
2	half chicken breasts, cooked and cubed*
1	green pepper, cut in strips
1	red pepper, cut in strips
1	yellow pepper, cut in strips
1	small can (10 oz.) pineapple chunks, drained
1	tablespoon sesame oil
1	tablespoon rice vinegar
1	teaspoon sugar
1	teaspoon Worcestershire sauce
¼	teaspoon cayenne pepper
1	bottle Kraft "Free" Catalina dressing (8 oz.)

To cook the wild rice, wash it well and put it in a pot that has a tight-fitting lid. Add 2¼ cups water. Bring to a boil, then reduce heat to low and cook, tightly covered, for 45 minutes. Remove from heat and let stand for 30 minutes. Stir lightly with a fork.

Place the cooked wild rice, chicken, peppers, and pineapple in a large bowl. In another bowl, mix the sesame oil, vinegar, sugar, Worcestershire sauce, and cayenne with the Catalina dressing. Add the dressing to the salad ingredients and mix gently together. Chill until serving time.

*Add a bit of lemon juice instead of salt to the water when poaching the chicken. You can oven poach by placing the chicken breasts in a small baking dish; add ½ cup water, cover tightly with aluminum foil, and bake in a 350° oven for 15 to 20 minutes.

Each serving provides:			
221	Calories	29 g	Carbohydrate
17 g	Protein	281 mg	Sodium
4 g	Fat	37 mg	Cholesterol

Elegant Chicken Mousse

This is a multipurpose dish. Perfect for an elegant lunch, it could also be served at a large cocktail party as a chicken pâté. After all, for anyone who has a cholesterol problem, liver pâté is history, right?
Serves 4 for lunch, or 10 to 12 as an appetizer.

1	whole chicken breast, cooked
½	cup red pepper, chopped
2	leeks, coarsely chopped (white part only)
1	teaspoon safflower or canola oil
⅔	cup chicken stock
1	envelope gelatin
1	carton low-fat cottage cheese (¾ cup)
1	tablespoon Dijon mustard
1	teaspoon lemon pepper
1	small container (6 oz.) low-fat yogurt
3	tablespoons fresh parsley, chopped
	No-stick vegetable oil spray

Remove the skin and bones from the chicken and cut the chicken into cubes. Put the red pepper and leeks into a food processor or blender and process until finely chopped. Heat the oil in a small skillet and sauté the pepper and leek mixture until soft (about 4 to 5 minutes). Set aside to cool. Pour the chicken broth into a small saucepan and sprinkle the gelatin over the top. Let this sit for 5 minutes, then heat over very low heat in a double boiler until the gelatin is dissolved. Let cool to lukewarm. Meanwhile, place the cubed chicken in the food processor and process until finely chopped. Add the cottage cheese, mustard, pepper, and yogurt and blend. With the motor still running, pour the gelatin mixture slowly into the food processor until blended. Stir in the sautéed pepper and leek mixture and the parsley. Spoon into a 4-cup mold which has been sprayed with a no-stick vegetable oil spray. Chill in the refrigerator for at least 4 hours, or until set. Unmold and serve on a plate lined with lettuce and garnished with sliced fruit.

Each lunch serving provides:			
255	Calories	14 g	Carbohydrate
34 g	Protein	863 mg	Sodium
7 g	Fat	49 mg	Cholesterol

Jellied Chicken Loaf

Wonderful summertime supper fare.

Serves 6.

2	chicken thighs
2	chicken drumsticks
1	whole chicken breast
4	cups water
1	teaspoon no-salt seasoning
1	medium onion, thickly sliced
1	slice unpeeled lemon
2	stalks celery, coarsely sliced
4	large cloves garlic
1	teaspoon summer savory
¼	teaspoon pepper
1	bay leaf
2	envelopes gelatin
3	tablespoons fresh parsley, chopped
	No-stick vegetable oil spray

Put all of the above ingredients (except the gelatin and parsley) into a Dutch oven or large pot. Bring to a boil. Reduce heat and simmer for 1 hour. Turn off heat and let the chicken cool in the broth for 2 to 2½ hours. Remove the chicken and whole garlic cloves from the broth. Strain the broth and set ½ cup aside. Return the remaining broth to the pot. Mash the garlic cloves and add to the pot. Sprinkle both packets of gelatin over the ½ cup of broth you set aside and let sit for 5 minutes. Remove the skin and all visible fat from the chicken; strip the meat from the bones and cut it into small pieces. Place the chopped chicken, along with the parsley, in a 9 × 5-inch loaf pan that has been sprayed with a no-stick vegetable oil spray. Heat the broth in the pot to boiling, and add the gelatin-broth mixture. Turn off heat and stir until gelatin is dissolved. Taste for seasoning. It might need a little salt, but no more than ¼ to ½ teaspoon. Pour the broth over the chicken and parsley. Push the meat around with a fork so the broth gets evenly distributed. Refrigerate, covered, until set (about 6 hours).

This is nice accompanied with lemon mayonnaise. (Stir 1 table-spoon fresh lemon juice and 1 teaspoon grated lemon rind into ½ cup of reduced-calorie mayonnaise.)

Each serving provides:			
117	Calories	3 g	Carbohydrate
20 g	Protein	79 mg	Sodium
2 g	Fat	58 mg	Cholesterol

Cold Glazed Chicken Breasts

Our friend Nicki served these last 4th of July. The centerpiece was a rectangular strawberry shortcake decorated with strawberries and blueberries to resemble the American flag. The dessert was a big hit — but so were the chicken breasts! (And they can be made the day before.)

Serves 8 to 10.

6	whole chicken breasts (skin and bone left on)
½	cup white wine
4	cups chicken stock
2	green onions, chopped
1	large carrot, sliced
1	celery stalk, sliced
1	bay leaf
¼	teaspoon thyme
4	sprigs fresh parsley
6	peppercorns
1	envelope gelatin
¼	cup white wine

Place the chicken in a Dutch oven or large saucepan and cover with the wine and chicken stock. Add all remaining ingredients except the gelatin and white wine. Bring to a boil. Reduce heat and simmer very gently for 10 minutes. Cover tightly, then turn off heat. Let the chicken sit in the broth to cool for a minimum of 3 hours. It can sit for as long as 6 hours, but after 4 hours it should be refrigerated.

Remove the cooled chicken from the broth and strain the broth to reserve for the glaze. Carefully remove the skin and bone from the breasts and chill the meat, covered, for 1 hour. Chill the broth as well. Remove congealed fat from the top of the chilled broth.

To prepare the glaze, sprinkle the gelatin over 1¼ cups of the cooled chicken broth in a small saucepan and stir to dissolve over medium heat. Add the ¼ cup white wine and chill in the refrigerator until thickened. When ready to serve, brush the breasts with the glaze and garnish with fresh parsley.

Each serving provides:			
201	Calories	2 g	Carbohydrate
38 g	Protein	136 mg	Sodium
3 g	Fat	91 mg	Cholesterol

Cold Breast of Chicken with Hot Pepper Jelly Sauce

Hot pepper jelly comes in both red (red pepper jelly) and green (jalapeño pepper jelly) — both are good.

Serves 4 to 6.

3   whole boneless chicken breasts, halved
¼   cup white wine

Remove the skin and all visible fat from the chicken breasts. Wash under cold running water and pat dry with paper towels. Place the chicken breasts in a baking dish and pour the wine over the top. Cover tightly with aluminum foil and bake in a preheated 350° oven for 20 minutes. Remove from the oven and allow to cool.

Serve at room temperature with the following sauce spooned on top:

Hot Pepper Jelly Sauce

½   cup hot pepper jelly
⅓   cup dry sherry
⅓   cup mild red chili sauce

Place the sauce ingredients in a small saucepan and heat over low heat until the jelly is melted. Serve at room temperature.

Each serving provides:			
234	Calories	23 g	Carbohydrate
28 g	Protein	284 mg	Sodium
2 g	Fat	68 mg	Cholesterol

Cold Breast of Chicken with Yogurt and Nut Sauce

Serves 4.

2	whole chicken breasts, skinned, boned, and halved
½	cup white wine or chicken stock
1	cup low-fat yogurt
2	tablespoons lemon juice
½	teaspoon ground cumin
4	tablespoons safflower oil
1	cup firmly packed fresh parsley, chopped
1	cup low-fat yogurt
½	cup pecans, chopped
	Freshly ground black pepper to taste
	Lemon slices and parsley for garnish

Remove any visible fat from the chicken breasts. Wash under cold running water and pat dry with paper towels. Place the chicken breasts in a baking dish and pour the wine (or stock) over the top. Cover tightly with aluminum foil and bake in a preheated 350° oven for 20 minutes. Remove from the oven and allow to cool to room temperature. Slice each breast into two or three pieces.

In a food processor or blender, combine the lemon juice, cumin, and oil. Blend well, and add the parsley, yogurt, nuts, and black pepper to taste. Blend again.

Pour the sauce over the chicken and put in the refrigerator to marinate overnight.

Serve on a large flat platter, garnished with lemon slices and parsley.

Each serving provides:

386	Calories	9 g	Carbohydrate
32 g	Protein	127 mg	Sodium
25 g	Fat*	72 mg	Cholesterol

---

*Although this is mostly the "good" type of fat, you may want to save this recipe for a special occasion.

Fruit-Stuffed Chicken Breasts with Warm Sherry Sauce

Serves 6.

3	whole chicken breasts, skinned, boned, and halved
½	cup chopped dried figs
½	cup chopped prunes
¼	cup chopped celery
½	small apple, chopped
1	tablespoon sherry
¼	teaspoon thyme

Pound the chicken breasts to ¼-inch thickness; they should be approximately twice their original size. In a small bowl, combine the remaining ingredients, mixing well. Spoon 1 generous tablespoon of the filling on each chicken breast and roll, folding the sides in as you go. Place seam-side down in a baking dish, in a single layer. Cover and bake in a preheated 325° oven for 30 minutes. Cool. Serve with the following sauce.

Warm Sherry Sauce

1	cup apple jelly
⅓	cup mild red chili sauce
¼	cup dry sherry

Combine the apple jelly and chili sauce in a small saucepan and cook over low heat until the jelly is melted. Stir in the sherry. Remove from heat and serve warm (or at room temperature) with the cold chicken.

Each serving provides:			
379	Calories	61 g	Carbohydrate
29 g	Protein	294 mg	Sodium
2 g	Fat	68 mg	Cholesterol

3

Barbecue

If you're wondering how skinless chicken will respond on the barbecue, the answer is — great! — particularly if you give it a head start in the microwave first.* Although precooking this way is not necessary, it does ensure a nice moist piece of chicken, while allowing you the pleasures of one of the most popular summer cooking methods. And, if you did miss the odd little bit of fat when cleaning your chicken, it will melt and drip off into the fire!

CHICKEN BARBECUING TIPS

Whenever using a grill, it's wise to assemble a few tools to simplify the cooking and make it safer. Long-handled metal spatulas and tongs are preferable to forks because they don't release the juices too soon. Large basting brushes speed application of sauce, and oven mitts are a much better choice than simple pot holders. Plastic squeeze bottles filled with water to extinguish flare-ups from drippings should be kept on hand, although our skinless, fatless chicken will not present too great a problem.

Here is a checklist we find helpful:

1. Clean the rack of charred buildup and grease with a wire brush before each use.

2. Season the rack by oiling it regularly.

3. Always preheat the barbecue before cooking — 10 minutes for gas and 30 to 40 minutes for charcoal, or until the coals have a layer of gray ash.

4. Lightly brush the hot rack with oil just before cooking to discourage food from sticking.

*To precook in the microwave: cover with wax paper and cook for 5 minutes per pound (1 pound for 5 minutes, 2 pounds for 10 minutes, etc.).

Barbecued Chicken Breasts

It's best to use boned chicken when barbecuing with a sauce that has any sugar, honey, or tomatoes in it — while the sauce may have a great flavor, it burns quite easily. Since boned chicken breasts take less time to cook than breasts with the bone in, burning is less likely.

Serves 3 to 4.

2	whole chicken breasts, skinned, boned, and halved
¼	cup low-sodium soy sauce
2	tablespoons mild red chili sauce
2	tablespoons honey
1	tablespoon olive oil
1	tablespoon green onion, chopped
2	cloves garlic, minced
1	teaspoon Worcestershire sauce
⅛	teaspoon Louisiana hot sauce

Flatten the chicken breasts slightly with a meat mallet (or the bottom of a small cast-iron frying pan) so the pieces will be of a fairly uniform thickness.

Combine all of the remaining ingredients. Pour the sauce over the chicken and marinate for 2 to 3 hours. Barbecue for about 3 to 4 minutes on each side. Because the chicken breast is off the bone and has been flattened, it won't take long to cook.

Each serving provides:

214	Calories	13 g	Carbohydrate
29 g	Protein	810 mg	Sodium
5 g	Fat	68 mg	Cholesterol

Mustard Chicken Breasts
with Red Pepper Jelly

This jelly is also lovely in a sandwich spread over cold sliced chicken and crisp lettuce.

Serves 3 to 4.

4	half chicken breasts, on the bone
1	teaspoon sweet Hungarian paprika
½	teaspoon lemon pepper
½	tablespoon French's mustard with onion bits*
3	tablespoons red wine vinegar
2	tablespoons soft margarine
1½	teaspoons water

Skin the chicken breasts and remove any visible fat. Combine the paprika and lemon pepper and rub into the chicken. Combine the remaining ingredients in a small saucepan and heat to boiling. Remove from heat. Brush on the chicken and place the chicken on a barbecue rack that has been brushed with oil. Cook for about 10 minutes on each side, basting frequently. Don't have heat too hot and don't overcook. Serve with the Red Pepper Jelly.

Red Pepper Jelly

2	small sweet red peppers, seeded, *finely* chopped
1½	cups sugar
6	tablespoons apple cider vinegar
½	package dry pectin

Combine the red peppers, sugar, and vinegar in a medium saucepan. Heat to boiling and boil for 10 minutes. Stir in the dry pectin and cook for 1 additional minute. Cool. Pour into a sterilized pint jar and store in the refrigerator.

*Dijon mustard may be substituted.

Each serving provides:			
578	Calories	84 g	Carbohydrate
25 g	Protein	310 mg	Sodium
17 g	Fat	76 mg	Cholesterol

Smokey Barbecued Chicken Breasts

Wonderful!

Serves 4.

1	medium onion, chopped
2	cloves garlic, minced
2	tablespoons olive oil
½	cup hot tea
¼	cup ketchup
2	tablespoons white wine vinegar
1	tablespoon honey
½	teaspoon Louisiana hot sauce
1	teaspoon liquid smoke
2	whole chicken breasts, skinned and halved

Sauté the onion and garlic in the olive oil until softened but not browned. Add all of the remaining ingredients except the chicken. Bring to a boil, reduce heat, and simmer uncovered for 10 minutes. Cool.

Place the chicken breasts in a shallow glass dish and pour the cooled sauce on top. Marinate, covered, in the refrigerator for up to 4 hours. Return to room temperature about 1 hour before cooking.

Preheat the barbecue. Just before cooking, brush the hot rack with oil. Remove the chicken from the marinade and cook for 5 to 10 minutes on each side over a medium-hot grill, basting frequently with the marinade. (Boil the marinade before using it for basting.) If the breasts are large, they might take a little bit longer to cook.

Each serving provides:

182	Calories	5 g	Carbohydrate
27 g	Protein	179 mg	Sodium
5 g	Fat	68 mg	Cholesterol

Plain and Simple Barbecued Chicken

If chicken burns on the grill before it is fully cooked, often it's because of the basting sauce. A basting sauce that contains sugar or tomatoes burns very easily and should be applied only during the last five or ten minutes of cooking time. Consequently, this type of sauce does little to keep the chicken moist. The basting sauce below will help keep barbecued chicken succulent since it can be used throughout the barbecuing process. If you use chicken halves instead of pieces, they will be juicier. You can cut them up after cooking. If the halves are small enough, you might find that those with larger appetites will have no trouble consuming an entire half.

Serves 8.

2   chickens, 2½ to 3 pounds each, split in half or cut into pieces
         with skin and all visible fat removed

Basting Sauce

½   cup safflower oil
½   cup white wine vinegar
¼   cup water
½   teaspoon no-salt seasoning

Combine the oil, vinegar, water, and no-salt seasoning.

Grease the grill while it is still cold by brushing lightly with vegetable oil, then place it 6 inches above the coals. When coals are ready, place the chicken on the grill, with the larger, meatier pieces in the center (where the heat is the greatest). Arrange the pieces close together to prevent heat from escaping through open spaces. Brush the basting sauce over the chicken and then baste every 5 minutes (turn every 8 to 10 minutes) until the chicken is done. Breasts will take 20 to 25 minutes, legs and thighs about 30 minutes (depending on size). Chicken halves will take a little longer, again depending on size.

Each serving provides:			
274	Calories	0 g	Carbohydrate
32 g	Protein	96 mg	Sodium
15 g	Fat*	99 mg	Cholesterol

*Although this is mostly the "good" type of fat, you may want to save this recipe for a special occasion.

Chutney Chicken Kabobs

The secret of great kabobs lies in the marinade. These kabobs are wonderfully easy to make because most of the preparation is done in advance and the actual cooking time is only a matter of minutes. Do not push the pieces of meat too closely together when threading or the meat will not cook evenly.

Serves 3 to 4.

1	pound boneless, skinless chicken breasts
½	teaspoon lemon pepper
½	cup mango chutney, coarsely chopped
⅓	cup white wine
1	tablespoon balsamic vinegar
½	red or green pepper, cut into chunks*
1	small onion, cut into chunks
	A few cherry tomatoes

Cut the chicken breasts into chunks and place in a bowl. Add the lemon pepper, chutney, white wine, and vinegar. Refrigerate for 6 hours or overnight. Remove chicken from the bowl and thread onto skewers alternately with the pieces of pepper, onion, and cherry tomatoes. Cook over low heat on the barbecue, or broil in the oven until the chicken is cooked, roughly 3 to 4 minutes on each side.

You can substitute chicken thighs for the breasts in this recipe very successfully. An advantage is that thighs are not as tricky to cook on the barbecue as far as timing. Overcooked breasts will be dry, but thighs can survive a bit of overcooking. However, it's more time consuming to bone and cut up the thighs — just another one of those good news–bad news cases!

*Chunks of zucchini may be substituted for the peppers.

Each serving provides:

174	Calories	12 g	Carbohydrate
27 g	Protein	159 mg	Sodium
1 g	Fat	66 mg	Cholesterol

Chicken Breasts with Red Pepper Salsa

This chicken can be cooked on the barbecue or sautéed. The sweet flavor of the salsa is a bit of a departure from traditional spicy salsas, but it goes very nicely with the chicken. You must roast the peppers since this is important to the flavor and texture of the sauce.

Serves 6.

3   whole chicken breasts, skinned, boned, and halved
¾   cup lemon juice

Combine the chicken breasts and lemon juice in a bowl just large enough to hold them comfortably. Cover and marinate in the refrigerator for 4 to 6 hours (all day is fine). Turn occasionally. Drain well.

Barbecue Method

No-stick vegetable oil spray

Grill the chicken on a grill sprayed with no-stick vegetable oil spray, about 6 to 7 inches away from the heat over very low heat. The chicken is cooked when it loses its pinkish color and is barely firm to the touch.

Each serving of chicken (barbecue method) provides:			
133	Calories	1 g	Carbohydrate
27 g	Protein	80 mg	Sodium
2 g	Fat	68 mg	Cholesterol

Sauté Method

½   cup flour
1   teaspoon paprika
1   teaspoon no-salt seasoning
½   teaspoon black pepper
2   tablespoons olive oil

Shake the drained chicken in a bag containing the flour, paprika, no-salt seasoning, and black pepper. (Brown paper bags are good for this purpose.) Sauté the chicken in a hot skillet with the olive oil. Cook for 3 minutes on each side or until golden brown and cooked through. (Do not overcook.)

Serve the chicken with a generous spoonful of the following salsa on the side.

Each serving of chicken (sauté method) provides:			
210	Calories	8 g	Carbohydrate
28 g	Protein	77 mg	Sodium
6 g	Fat	68 mg	Cholesterol

Red Pepper Salsa

2	red bell peppers
1	green bell pepper
4	medium tomatoes, seeded and chopped
4	green onions, finely chopped
	Pinch of cayenne pepper
2	tablespoons cilantro, chopped
6	tablespoons red wine vinegar
4	tablespoons white sugar

To roast the peppers, place them under the broiler, turning at intervals until blistered and *slightly* charred all over (this takes about 10 minutes). Put the peppers in a brown paper bag or plastic bag and seal well. Let the peppers "steam" in the bag for about 10 minutes, then peel off the skin with a sharp knife. Cut in half, remove the seeds, and chop. (Once you see how relatively simple it is to roast peppers and what a distinctively different flavor results, you'll become an enthusiast. Peppers may also be roasted on the barbecue. Peeled and dressed with a nice vinaigrette, they make a wonderful side salad.)

Drain the tomatoes well and put into a mixing bowl with the peppers, green onions, cayenne, and cilantro. In a small skillet, mix the vinegar and sugar and cook until they start to form a thin syrup and begin to caramelize — about 3 to 5 minutes over high heat. Add to the tomato-pepper mixture. For the freshest flavor, this is best made the day of serving. Salsas are one of the freshest ways to dress grilled meats.

Each serving of salsa provides:			
62	Calories	15 g	Carbohydrate
1 g	Protein	8 mg	Sodium
0 g	Fat	0 mg	Cholesterol

Cajun Chicken Kabobs

If you don't have time to marinate chicken (which is preferable for kabobs) we suggest you serve the kabobs with the following sauce. Brush the sauce on the chicken just before removing from the grill to avoid burning. Pass extra sauce at the table. These kabobs can also be broiled in the oven.

Serves 6.

2	pounds boneless, skinless chicken breasts
8	bamboo or metal skewers*

Cajun Sauce

1	can (7½ oz.) tomato sauce
1	tablespoon chili powder
1	teaspoon white wine vinegar
¼	teaspoon crushed red pepper
¼	teaspoon Louisiana hot sauce
1	teaspoon brown sugar
⅓	cup chicken stock (or water)

Place all sauce ingredients into a small saucepan and blend well. Simmer over low heat for about 5 minutes. Set aside and keep warm, or reheat just before serving.

Cut the chicken into 1 to 1½-inch pieces. Divide equally among 8 skewers. When threading the chicken onto the skewers, don't place too close together or the pieces won't cook evenly. Grill until the chicken is cooked (approximately 3 to 4 minutes on each side).

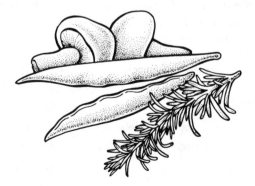

Brush a small amount of Cajun sauce over the chicken for the last
minute of cooking. Watch the chicken carefully. Chicken breasts
dry out very quickly when exposed to high heat. Serve the kabobs
with extra sauce on the side.

*If using bamboo skewers, soak in cold water at least 1 hour before thread-
ing the chicken to help prevent burning during barbecuing.

Each serving provides:			
186	Calories	4 g	Carbohydrate
36 g	Protein	334 mg	Sodium
2 g	Fat	88 mg	Cholesterol

Mushroom Chicken Kabobs with Yogurt Sauce

This is informal but fun barbecue fare for lazy summer suppers. It might be called "stir fry on a stick"! A novel and very casual way of serving these would be to have a plate of shredded lettuce and some pita bread ready. Place some lettuce in a pita pocket, then the hot chicken and vegetables, and top with the Yogurt Sauce.

Serves 3 to 4.

1	pound boneless, skinless chicken breasts
¼	cup sesame oil
¼	cup water
¼	cup vermouth
3	tablespoons low-sodium soy sauce
¼	teaspoon powdered ginger
1	clove garlic, minced
½	pound fresh mushrooms
½	red or green pepper, cut into chunks
1	small raw onion, cut into chunks

Cut the chicken into chunks. Combine the oil, water, vermouth, soy sauce, ginger, and garlic in a large bowl. Marinate the chicken in this mixture for at least 1 hour. Just before you are ready to assemble the kabobs, pour boiling water over the mushrooms and let them sit a minute or two. This will prevent splitting when you insert them onto a skewer. Thread the mushrooms alternately with the chicken, peppers, and onion and cook over low heat on the barbecue (or broil in the oven) until the chicken is cooked — roughly 3 to 4 minutes on each side. Serve with the following sauce.

Each serving of chicken provides:			
219	Calories	4 g	Carbohydrate
28 g	Protein	302 mg	Sodium
9 g	Fat	66 mg	Cholesterol

Yogurt Sauce

1   cup low-fat yogurt
⅓   cup green onions, sliced
2   tablespoons fresh parsley, finely chopped
1   small tomato, seeded and diced

Combine all of the sauce ingredients in a small bowl. (Don't use dried parsley flakes in this recipe — the flavor won't be right.)

Each serving of yogurt sauce provides:			
43	Calories	6 g	Carbohydrate
3 g	Protein	43 mg	Sodium
1 g	Fat	3 mg	Cholesterol

Barbecued Chicken Tandoori Style

This dish is reminiscent of Indian tandoori cooked chicken. The tandoor is a cylindrical clay oven that cooks food over charcoal. Some rice pilaf and a raita (a cucumber and yogurt salad)* would be excellent accompaniments.

Serves 6 to 8.

3-3½ pounds chicken parts, skinned**

Marinade

1	small carton (6 oz.) low-fat yogurt
½	teaspoon fresh ginger, grated
1	large clove garlic, minced
2	tablespoons fresh lemon juice
2	teaspoons curry powder
¼	teaspoon cinnamon
½	teaspoon salt
¼	teaspoon crushed red pepper

Combine all of the marinade ingredients and spoon over the chicken pieces, mixing well. Refrigerate all day or overnight.

Remove the chicken from the marinade and barbecue about 6 inches from the hot coals, turning as necessary to prevent burning. Breasts (if they are from a small chicken) will take about 10 minutes on each side, legs and thighs will take anywhere from 30 to 40 minutes, depending on the size of the chicken and intensity of heat (keep in mind, too, that it's hotter with the hood down). It's best not to have the heat too high.

*To make the raita, peel and grate an English cucumber into a bowl and mix in 1 cup low-fat yogurt, ½ teaspoon powdered cumin, ⅛ to ¼ teaspoon black pepper, and ¼ teaspoon salt. Garnish with a few cilantro leaves.

**Remember that white meat has less fat than dark. We know you can't have a steady diet of white meat, but keep the thought!

Each serving provides:			
137	Calories	2 g	Carbohydrate
24 g	Protein	212 mg	Sodium
3 g	Fat	71 mg	Cholesterol

Slimmer's Grilled Chicken

Serves 3 to 4.

3-4 half chicken breasts, skinned and boned
⅓   cup fresh lemon juice
¼   cup low-sodium soy sauce
1   clove garlic, minced
¼   teaspoon powdered ginger
2   teaspoons tarragon
     No-stick vegetable oil spray

Pound the chicken breasts gently between two pieces of plastic wrap until they are a uniform thickness (they will cook faster and flavors will penetrate more evenly). Place in a shallow dish. Combine the remaining ingredients and pour over the chicken. Marinate for a minimum of 4 hours (all day or even overnight is fine, but refrigerate if you do this). Turn once or twice during the marinating process.

When ready to cook, spray the grill well with no-stick vegetable oil spray and grill the chicken until cooked (about 3 minutes on each side). Timing will depend on the thickness of the chicken and the heat of the coals. Use your best judgment but don't overcook the chicken or it will dry out.

Note: These can be broiled in the oven as well.

	Each serving provides:		
141	Calories	2 g	Carbohydrate
28 g	Protein	389 mg	Sodium
2 g	Fat	68 mg	Cholesterol

Chicken with Spicy Barbecue Sauce

Serve the leftover barbecue sauce in a separate dish in case anyone wants more. It's not too spicy — we think it's just right. It's also a lot more economical to make your own barbecue sauce than to buy it.

Serves 4 to 5.

3-3½ pounds chicken pieces, skinned

Spicy Barbecue Sauce

¾   cup tomato juice
¼   cup "hot" ketchup
¼   cup water
¼   cup white wine vinegar
2   tablespoons Worcestershire sauce
2   tablespoons brown sugar
1½ teaspoons dry mustard
1   teaspoon no-salt seasoning
1   tablespoon paprika
⅛   teaspoon cayenne pepper

Combine all of the barbecue sauce ingredients in a small saucepan and bring to a boil. Boil slowly, stirring occasionally until the sauce is slightly thickened. (Makes about 1½ cups.)

Wash the chicken pieces and pat dry. (If you have a microwave, place the chicken in it for 5 to 8 minutes, depending on the size of the pieces. Your chicken will be moister than that cooked the whole time on the grill.) Start basting the chicken with barbecue sauce when it's about halfway done. (Any sauce with sugar in it tends to burn if it cooks for too long.)

Cooking time for barbecued chicken parts is about 35 to 40 minutes on an open grill. A covered grill will take less time, around 30 minutes. If you start the chicken in the microwave, reduce the cooking time by half. Remember that breasts cook faster than legs and thighs.

Each serving provides:			
298	Calories	11 g	Carbohydrate
39 g	Protein	401 mg	Sodium
10 g	Fat	117 mg	Cholesterol

Lemonade Barbecued Chicken

This might sound like an odd combination but it's quite delicious. This recipe also works well when broiled in your oven. Because of the sugar content in the lemonade, the chicken has a tendency to burn at too high a heat, so watch carefully. You'll be rewarded!

Serves 6 to 8.

1	can (6 oz.) frozen lemonade concentrate, thawed
1	teaspoon celery seed
¼	cup low-sodium soy sauce
1	teaspoon garlic powder
4	whole chicken breasts, skinned, boned, and halved

Combine the lemonade, celery seed, soy sauce, and garlic powder. Marinate the chicken in this for 4 to 8 hours. Drain the marinade and grill the chicken 6 to 7 inches from the coals on very low heat until the chicken loses its pinkish color and is browned and tender. Turn only once.

To oven broil: Place the chicken under the broiler and cook on medium-low heat for 4 to 5 minutes on each side. You can judge the intensity of the broiler heat by using the following "hand test." If you can hold your hand under the heat for 2 seconds, it's hot; 3 seconds, it's medium-high; 4 seconds, it's medium; and 5 seconds, it's low.

Each serving provides:			
172	Calories	11 g	Carbohydrate
28 g	Protein	306 mg	Sodium
2 g	Fat	68 mg	Cholesterol

Dunking Drumsticks

Great for a backyard barbecue. The sauce is so good you may be tempted to eat it with a spoon! It keeps well in the refrigerator, up to four weeks. It may seem expensive when you're gathering the ingredients, but it makes almost 2 quarts and can be used for any meat you barbecue. Great on hamburgers (make sure you use the leanest ground round) or try substituting ground turkey for ground beef. You'll find that turkey burgers, especially when basted with this great sauce, make fine barbecue fare.

Serves 8 to 10.

6	pounds small chicken drumsticks (roughly 24)
	No-stick vegetable oil spray

Barbecue Sauce

2	tablespoons soft margarine
2	tablespoons safflower oil
1	medium onion, finely chopped
1	large bottle (16 oz.) barbecue sauce
1	cup beer
1	jar (8 oz.) orange marmalade
1	teaspoon liquid smoke
2	tablespoons molasses
2	tablespoons Worcestershire sauce
2	tablespoons lemon juice
½	teaspoon ground cloves

Heat the margarine and oil in a large saucepan or Dutch oven and sauté the onion until it is soft and just starts to turn color (don't brown). Add all the remaining sauce ingredients and simmer slowly, covered, for about 45 minutes, stirring occasionally. Remove the cover for the last 15 minutes if the sauce is not thick enough.

Spray the barbecue grill with the no-stick vegetable oil spray and put the drumsticks on the grill, basting with the sauce only during the last 5 minutes. We like to precook the drumsticks in the microwave for roughly 8 to 10 minutes to keep them from drying out.

Each serving provides:

267	Calories	9 g	Carbohydrate
39 g	Protein	300 mg	Sodium
9 g	Fat	141 mg	Cholesterol

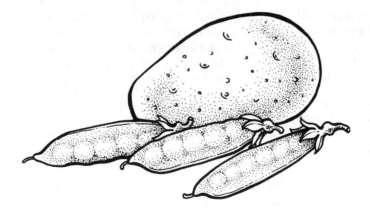

Overnight Barbecued Chicken

This recipe never fails to please. If you want your thighs super tender, give them about 8 minutes in the microwave first.

Serves 6 to 8.

3-3½   pounds (about 8 to 10) small to medium chicken thighs
¾   cup white wine
2-3   tablespoons olive oil
¼   cup low-sodium soy sauce
2   cloves garlic, minced
2   tablespoons Dijon mustard*
2   tablespoons lemon juice
        Freshly ground black pepper to taste

Remove the skin and all visible fat from the thighs. Wash with cold water and dry with paper towels. Place in a deep glass or ceramic bowl.

Combine all of the remaining ingredients and pour over the thighs. Allow to marinate overnight. Baste often while barbecuing.

It's difficult to give precise timing for barbecued chicken since there are so many variables. The size of the chicken pieces, the temperature of the barbecue, and the proximity of the grill to the coals are the major points to consider when determining cooking time. Small thighs could take anywhere from 20 to 30 minutes. It's best to insert a small sharp knife close to the bone to check for doneness after 20 minutes. Turn the chicken every 10 minutes.

*Dijon mustard can be very high in sodium; if you're watching your salt intake, substitute a low-salt or salt-free mustard.

Each serving provides:			
124	Calories	2 g	Carbohydrate
14 g	Protein	474 mg	Sodium
6 g	Fat	57 mg	Cholesterol

4

The Stovetop: Sautés, Stews, and More

For those of us who love to cook, the stovetop method of preparing meals gives a sense of enjoyment and fulfillment. Sautéeing, stirring, whisking, and browning are all part of the hands-on approach to cooking that we love.

For those who cook for a more pragmatic reasons — to put a nutritious, well-balanced meal on the table — stovetop cooking offers benefits to you as well. It's speedy and controllable — and it fills the kitchen with wonderful aromas.

So, whether you love to cook or have to cook, we know you'll enjoy our stovetop recipes. They've all been specially developed for excellent results.

Amaretto Chicken

Serves 8.

8	half chicken breasts, boneless or on the bone
	No-stick vegetable oil spray
2	tablespoons oat bran
1	cup chicken stock
½	cup low-fat evaporated milk
2	tablespoons Amaretto
	Lemon pepper to taste

Remove the skin from the breasts. Spray a large skillet well with no-stick vegetable oil spray and brown the chicken breasts. Sprinkle the breasts with oat bran as they brown. Add the chicken stock. Bring to a boil and cover. Turn heat immediately to low and simmer gently for 15 minutes if the breasts are boneless, for 20 to 25 minutes if the bone is in, or until the chicken is done. Remove the chicken to a heated serving dish and add the evaporated milk to the skillet. Return to a boil and cook over high heat, stirring constantly until the sauce is reduced to a thick, creamy consistency. Stir in the Amaretto. Remove from heat and spoon the sauce over the chicken breasts. Add lemon pepper to taste.

Each serving provides:			
162	Calories	4 g	Carbohydrate
29 g	Protein	100 mg	Sodium
2 g	Fat	71 mg	Cholesterol

Chicken with Apples and Cider

Whoever coined the phrase "an apple a day keeps the doctor away" was right on target. While eating a fresh apple is preferable, cooked ones are also beneficial (and delicious).

Serves 4.

	No-stick vegetable oil cooking spray
2½-3	pounds chicken parts, skin and all traces of fat removed
2	tablespoons oat bran
1	cup apple cider
	No-salt seasoning and freshly ground pepper to taste
½	teaspoon thyme
2	tart apples, peeled, cored, and cut into quarters
½	cup low-fat evaporated milk

Spray a 12-inch Teflon skillet well with no-stick vegetable oil spray. Heat the skillet and brown the chicken on all sides, sprinkling with the oat bran while it is browning. Add the cider, no-salt seasoning, pepper, and thyme. Cover and simmer until the chicken is almost cooked (roughly 25 minutes). Add the apples and simmer about 5 more minutes, or until the apples and chicken are cooked. Transfer the chicken and apples to a warm platter and keep warm. Add the evaporated milk to the pan juices and boil, stirring constantly, until the sauce is reduced and thickened. Spoon the sauce over the chicken and serve.

Each serving provides:			
280	Calories	22 g	Carbohydrate
35 g	Protein	150 mg	Sodium
6 g	Fat	110 mg	Cholesterol

Chicken with Apricot Sauce

Lots of good apricot sauce to spoon over chicken breasts and hot, fluffy rice.

Serves 6 to 8.

1	tablespoon cornstarch
2	cups apricot nectar
2	teaspoons chicken bouillon mix*
½	teaspoon dry mustard
⅛	teaspoon no-salt seasoning
2	tablespoons white wine vinegar
¾	cup apricot jam
8	half chicken breasts, skinned and boned

Dissolve the cornstarch in ½ cup of the apricot nectar in a medium-sized saucepan. Add the remaining nectar, chicken bouillon mix, dry mustard, no-salt seasoning, and vinegar. Stir over medium to high heat until the mixture starts to boil and thicken. Stir in the apricot jam and remove from heat when the jam is melted. Cool.

Place the chicken breasts in a single layer in a large skillet and pour the sauce on top. Cover and refrigerate for at least 4 hours (or overnight). Half an hour before serving, remove the skillet from the refrigerator and simmer the chicken in the sauce (uncovered), over medium heat, until the chicken is tender. Spoon the sauce over the chicken from time to time while cooking. The sauce will thicken and the chicken should be cooked in 15 to 20 minutes.

*Chicken bouillon mix is usually rather high in salt. Readers on salt-restricted diets may want to skip this recipe, or try it without the bouillon.

Each serving provides:			
253	Calories	31 g	Carbohydrate
28 g	Protein	323 mg	Sodium
2 g	Fat	68 mg	Cholesterol

Honey Lemon Chicken Breasts

Serve with orange slices and brown rice.

Serves 4.

4	half chicken breasts
2	tablespoons canola or safflower oil
½	teaspoon cinnamon
¼	cup honey
¼	cup lemon juice
½	cup white wine

Brown the chicken breasts in the oil in a large skillet. Stir the cinnamon into the honey and coat the breasts with this mixture. Add the lemon juice and wine to the skillet. Cover and simmer for 20 to 25 minutes for boneless breasts and 30 to 35 minutes for breasts with the bone in.

Each serving provides:

259	Calories	19 g	Carbohydrate
27 g	Protein	82 mg	Sodium
8 g	Fat	68 mg	Cholesterol

David's Lemon Mushroom Chicken Breasts

The wonderful lemon-sherry flavor combination more than makes up for the lack of salt in this recipe.

Serves 3 to 4.

2	whole chicken breasts, boned, skinned, and halved
	No-stick vegetable oil spray
2	tablespoons soft margarine
¼	cup green onions, sliced
1	cup fresh mushrooms, sliced
4	very thin slices of fresh lemon, cut into quarters*
2	tablespoons fresh lemon juice
2	tablespoons dry sherry

Wash the chicken breasts under cold running water and dry with paper towels. Remove any pieces of cartilage and any visible fat. Flatten the breasts with a mallet or the bottom of a frying pan — just enough to achieve a uniform thickness so they will cook evenly. Spray a medium-sized Teflon frying pan with no-stick vegetable oil spray and sauté the chicken breasts for about 2 to 3 minutes on each side (you want it cooked through but not dry). Remove to a warm platter and keep warm. Melt the margarine in the same pan. Add the onions and the mushrooms and sauté over high heat until the mushrooms are soft. Add the 16 lemon pieces, and then the lemon juice and sherry. Bring to a boil. When the liquid has reduced and is almost glazelike in appearance, remove from heat and spoon over the chicken breasts.

*Use a thin-skinned lemon (lemons with thick rinds tend to be bitter). With a very sharp knife cut the lemon into thin rounds, and then slice each round into quarters.

Each serving provides:			
193	Calories	3 g	Carbohydrate
28 g	Protein	155 mg	Sodium
7 g	Fat	68 mg	Cholesterol

Sherry Drumsticks

Serves 4.

	No-stick vegetable oil cooking spray
8	drumsticks, skinned
4	teaspoons oat bran
1	cup chicken stock
¼	cup dry sherry
2	tablespoons fresh parsley, chopped

Spray a 10-inch Teflon skillet well with the no-stick vegetable oil spray. Heat the skillet and brown the chicken, sprinkling with the oat bran on both sides while browning. When the drumsticks have browned, add the stock and bring to a boil. Cover and reduce heat to simmer. Cook until the chicken is tender (about 25 minutes for fryer drumsticks). Remove the cover and add the sherry. Bring to a boil and cook over high heat until the sauce is reduced to a creamy consistency. Remove to a serving dish and sprinkle with the fresh parsley.

Each serving provides:			
171	Calories	4 g	Carbohydrate
27 g	Protein	125 mg	Sodium
5 g	Fat	95 mg	Cholesterol

Onion Marmalade Chicken Breasts

*We served this dish to a well-travelled friend who swears he had a
similar dish in Paris last year. Make the Onion Marmalade ahead of time.*

Serves 2.

2	half chicken breasts, skinned
	No-salt seasoning
	Freshly ground black pepper
	Paprika
1	tablespoon olive oil
	Fresh parsley or tarragon leaves

Season the chicken lightly with the no-salt seasoning, pepper,
and paprika. Heat the olive oil and brown the chicken lightly on
all sides for 3 to 5 minutes. Cover and cook *gently* over low heat
for an additional 10 minutes, or until the meat is firm to the touch.
You want the meat cooked but still very tender. Transfer to individual serving plates. Spoon a serving of the onion marmalade on
each plate. Garnish the chicken with fresh parsley or, better still,
fresh tarragon leaves, if available.

Onion Marmalade

3	tablespoons olive oil
1	pound onions, finely sliced (about 3 medium onions)
3½	tablespoons brown sugar
2	tablespoons rice wine vinegar

Warm the olive oil in a small, *heavy-bottomed* saucepan. Add the
onions and stir well until the onions are coated with oil. Stir in the
sugar. Bring the mixture to a boil; immediately turn to simmer and

cook, covered, stirring occasionally, for 1½ hours. Stir in the rice wine vinegar until it is well absorbed. Continue to simmer, uncovered this time, for an additional 30 minutes. The mixture will have a marmalade-like appearance. Cool and store in the refrigerator. Serve cold.

Note: This recipe doubles well.

Each serving provides:			
538	Calories	40 g	Carbohydrate
30 g	Protein	91 mg	Sodium
29 g	Fat*	68 mg	Cholesterol

*We know this looks high in fat, but it's actually a lower-fat version than the original — save it for special occasions.

Burnt Onion Chicken

This dish makes a dramatic presentation, with dark brown, almost black, onions against the white flesh of the chicken. The flavors blend wonderfully. Don't overcook the chicken; you want the breasts moist, not dried out. You need a cast-iron frying pan to cook the onions.

Serves 2.

1   small to medium onion, peeled, thinly sliced, and pushed
     into rings
2   tablespoons soft margarine
2   half chicken breasts, skinned and boned
     Lemon pepper

Cook the onion in a cast-iron frying pan over high heat for 5 minutes, stirring frequently. Lower heat to medium and continue to cook, stirring constantly for an additional 3 to 5 minutes or until deep black-brown (but not carbonized for then they will be too bitter). Set aside.

Heat a non-stick skillet over medium heat and add the margarine. When the margarine is melted, add the chicken breasts, which you have sprinkled lightly with lemon pepper. Press the breasts lightly with a spatula to encourage even browning. Cook for 3 minutes. Turn and cook the other side for an additional 3 to 4 minutes (depending on the size of the breast), or until done. (A small sharp knife inserted in the thickest part will determine whether a trace of pink still remains.) Serve at once topped with the burnt onions.

Each serving provides:

242	Calories	2 g	Carbohydrate
28 g	Protein	230 mg	Sodium
13 g	Fat*	68 mg	Cholesterol

---

*We know this looks high in fat, but it's actually a lower-fat version than the original — save it for special occasions.

Salsa Chicken Breasts

This is one chicken dish that's hot even when it's cold!

Serves 4.

4	half chicken breasts, skinned and boned
⅓	cup flour
½	teaspoon garlic powder
½	teaspoon paprika
½	teaspoon chili powder
2	tablespoons safflower or canola oil
¼	cup Mexican-style tomato salsa
½	cup low-fat mozzarella cheese, grated

Place each chicken breast between two pieces of plastic wrap and flatten to ½ to ¼ inch thick with a mallet or the bottom of a wine bottle. Combine the flour, garlic powder, paprika, and chili powder. Coat the chicken with the flour mixture. Heat the oil in a large skillet over medium-high heat. Brown the chicken on both sides until no longer pink in the center. (This will only take 2 to 3 minutes, depending on the thickness of the chicken.) Reduce heat and spoon 1 tablespoon salsa onto the center of each chicken piece. Sprinkle evenly with the cheese. Cover and cook gently until the cheese is melted. If you like it spicy, serve with additional salsa on the side.

Each serving provides:			
271	Calories	10 g	Carbohydrate
32 g	Protein	236 mg	Sodium
11 g	Fat	77 mg	Cholesterol

Chicken Breasts with Green Peppercorn Sauce

Serves 4 to 6.

2	tablespoons dried green peppercorns
¼	cup hot water
½	teaspoon garlic powder
4-6	half chicken breasts, skinned and boned
2	tablespoons canola oil or safflower oil
¼	cup flour
⅓	cup low-fat evaporated milk
1	cup chicken stock (if using canned, use a low-sodium brand)

Soak the peppercorns in the hot water for 10 minutes. Sprinkle the garlic powder over the chicken. Heat the oil in a skillet and sauté the chicken until lightly browned. Sprinkle the flour over the chicken and sauté until all the flour is incorporated into the pan juices. Add the evaporated milk, stock, and peppercorns, along with the water in which they were soaking. Bring to a boil. Reduce heat and simmer gently for 10 to 15 minutes.

Each serving provides:			
226	Calories	8 g	Carbohydrate
30 g	Protein	237 mg	Sodium
7 g	Fat	71 mg	Cholesterol

Chicken Schnitzel for Two

You can make this for more than two by doubling or tripling the proportions. Make sure you have enough lemon wedges to do this. Fresh lemon juice squeezed over the chicken just before eating makes this dish for us.

Serves 2.

1   teaspoon fresh lemon juice
2   half chicken breasts, skinned and boned
1   egg white
1   teaspoon water
2   tablespoons Parmesan cheese
4   tablespoons cornflake crumbs
1   tablespoon olive oil
    Freshly ground black pepper
    Fresh lemon wedges

Drizzle the lemon juice over the chicken breasts. In a small bowl lightly beat the egg white and water together. Spread the Parmesan cheese on a flat plate or piece of wax paper; spread the cornflake crumbs on another. Coat the chicken breasts with the cheese, then with the egg white mixture, and finally with the cornflake crumbs, coating both sides evenly. Lay them on a rack and refrigerate, uncovered, for 30 minutes. Heat the olive oil in a heavy skillet over moderately high heat for 1 minute. Add the chicken and brown for about 3 minutes on each side, or until no longer pink when cut near the center. Add black pepper to taste. Serve the chicken garnished with plenty of fresh lemon wedges and perhaps a sprig of basil.

Each serving provides:			
282	Calories	16 g	Carbohydrate
33 g	Protein	373 mg	Sodium
10 g	Fat	72 mg	Cholesterol

Rosemary Chicken

Serves 6.

6   half chicken breasts, skinned and boned
       Freshly ground black pepper
1½   teaspoons dried rosemary
2   tablespoons canola or safflower oil
¼   cup dry white wine
½   cup low-fat evaporated milk

Pound the chicken breasts between two pieces of plastic wrap until they reach an even thickness (about ¼ to ½ inch). Dust both sides of each breast with the black pepper and crumbled rosemary. In a heavy skillet, heat the oil over medium-high heat and sauté the chicken until it's golden brown on both sides and no longer pink in the center. (Don't overcook; these pieces need only 2 to 3 minutes on each side.) Remove from the pan and keep warm. Deglaze the pan with the white wine. Reduce heat and stir in the evaporated milk. Continue to cook the sauce until bubbly and slightly thickened. Pour over the chicken.

Each serving provides:			
196	Calories	2 g	Carbohydrate
29 g	Protein	99 mg	Sodium
6 g	Fat	72 mg	Cholesterol

Simple Chicken Sauté for Two

Dishes as simple as this can look and taste as if they were prepared by a professional. Serve it with wild rice and fresh asparagus. Lightly sautéed cherry tomatoes would be another good addition.

Serves 2.

2	half chicken breasts, skinned and boned
1	tablespoon olive oil
1½	tablespoons green onions, chopped
4	mushrooms, chopped
2	tablespoons fresh lemon juice
1	tablespoon soft margarine
2	teaspoons fresh parsley, chopped

Rinse the chicken, remove all visible fat, and dry thoroughly with paper towels. Flatten slightly with the heel of your hand to attain a uniform thickness for even cooking. Heat the olive oil in a 10-inch skillet. Sauté the chicken for 3 minutes on each side, or until just firm to the touch. Remove the chicken from the pan and keep warm. Using the same skillet, sauté the green onions until translucent. Add the mushrooms and cook for about 2 minutes. Stir in the lemon juice and boil until most of the liquid has evaporated. Stir in the soft margarine. Spoon this mixture over the chicken breasts and sprinkle the parsley on top.

Note: 1 tablespoon drained capers may be added when you add the lemon juice. Not everyone likes capers, but if you do, they definitely add interest to this dish. Fresh spinach and a broiled tomato would be good accompaniments if you add the capers.

Each serving provides:			
255	Calories	3 g	Carbohydrate
28 g	Protein	155 mg	Sodium
14 g	Fat*	68 mg	Cholesterol

*Although this is mostly the "good" type of fat, you may want to save this recipe for a special occasion.

Chicken Shoyu

Serves 4.

2½-3 pounds chicken parts, skin and all visible fat removed
2   tablespoons flour
1   teaspoon powdered ginger
       No-stick vegetable oil spray
¼   cup low-sodium soy sauce
½   cup water
2   tablespoons red wine vinegar
¼   cup brown sugar
1   can (8 oz.) crushed pineapple, drained

Wash the chicken under cold running water and dry well with paper towels. Dust the chicken with the flour, then rub with the ginger. Spray a large Teflon frying pan well with the no-stick vegetable oil spray and brown the chicken on both sides. Combine the soy sauce, water, vinegar, and brown sugar. Pour over the chicken. Spoon the crushed pineapple on top. Bring to a boil. Cover the chicken, turn heat down to simmer, and cook the chicken until tender (30 to 40 minutes). Baste occasionally during this time.
Serve over rice.

Each serving provides:

292	Calories	27 g	Carbohydrate
34 g	Protein	720 mg	Sodium
5 g	Fat	105 mg	Cholesterol

Sweet Red Pepper Chicken

The chicken can be marinated the night before, or in the morning, making it a fairly simple dish to prepare even on a busy day. It's a lovely, moist, flavorful dish that needs nothing more than some steamed rice and a green salad.

Serves 4.

2	tablespoons low-sodium soy sauce
1½	teaspoons sage
3	cloves garlic, minced
¼	teaspoon black pepper
1¾	cups white wine
2½-3	pounds chicken, cut into pieces, skin and all visible fat removed
1	tablespoon soft margarine
1	tablespoon olive oil
1	cup onion, coarsely chopped
1	cup sweet red pepper, coarsely chopped (1 large pepper)
2	tablespoons chutney (tomato or mango)*

In a medium-sized bowl, mix the soy sauce, sage, garlic, pepper, and wine. Add the chicken pieces and marinate for at least 2 hours.

Drain the chicken pieces well, but *reserve* the marinade. In a large skillet with a lid, or an electric frying pan, sauté the chicken pieces in the margarine and olive oil until the chicken is nicely browned. Remove the chicken to a small platter and add the chopped onion and red pepper to the skillet. Sauté until the onion is soft. Stir the chutney into the reserved marinade and add to the skillet. Turn heat up to high and boil liquid until it is reduced to half its original volume (roughly 8 to 10 minutes). Turn heat off. Add the chicken and spoon some of the sauce over the chicken pieces. Return to a boil. Cover tightly and lower heat to simmer for 30 to 35 minutes, or until the chicken is tender.

*Major Grey brand chutney is excellent if you can find it.

Each serving provides:			
287	Calories	12 g	Carbohydrate
34 g	Protein	478 mg	Sodium
11 g	Fat	105 mg	Cholesterol

Chicken with Tomatoes and Artichoke Hearts

Serves 4.

2½-3 pounds chicken, cut into pieces
        No stick vegetable oil spray
¼   cup oat bran
1   teaspoon garlic powder (or 1 clove garlic, minced)
1   teaspoon no-salt seasoning
        Freshly ground pepper to taste
1   teaspoon dried basil
¼   teaspoon dried oregano
1   can (14 oz.) stewed tomatoes, broken up with a fork
1   can (14 oz.) artichoke hearts, drained

Remove the skin and all visible fat from the chicken pieces.
Spray a 10-inch Teflon frying pan with the no-stick vegetable oil
spray. Brown the chicken over medium heat, sprinkling with oat
bran on both sides as it browns. Sprinkle the garlic powder fairly
liberally over the top. Season with the no-salt seasoning, pepper,
basil, and oregano. Add the tomatoes and the artichoke hearts.
Bring to a boil. Cover, reduce heat, and cook for 30 minutes. Serve
over hot pasta or rice.

Each serving provides:			
253	Calories	17 g	Carbohydrate
36 g	Protein	401 mg	Sodium
6 g	Fat	105 mg	Cholesterol

French Canadian Chicken Bouillon

This half soup–half stew is the ultimate comfort food, but you must include the summer savory — no other herb quite does it. This stew has been warming hearts on cold nights in eastern Canada for centuries. It's traditionally served in old-fashioned soup plates. Eat this with a spoon plus a knife and fork.

Serves 4.

1   whole chicken (2-3 pounds), cut into pieces and skinned
    No-salt seasoning and pepper to taste*
1   large onion, cut into quarters
2   large potatoes, peeled and cut into quarters
3   large carrots, cut into large chunks
1   heaping teaspoon summer savory
    Fresh parsley, chopped (optional)

Place the chicken in a Dutch oven and almost cover with cold water. Add the no-salt seasoning and pepper to taste. Add the onion to the pot. Bring to a boil. Reduce heat to simmer and cook the chicken about 40 to 45 minutes, or until tender. Add the potatoes and carrots and continue to cook for 25 to 30 minutes, or until the vegetables are tender. Add the summer savory (this is the secret to this recipe). Serve portions of the chicken along with some vegetables and the broth in large soup plates or bowls. If you like, sprinkle chopped fresh parsley on top.

This is wonderful with fresh-from-the-oven homemade rolls or bread.

*A combination of salt and no-salt seasoning may be used.

Each serving provides:			
315	Calories	31 g	Carbohydrate
36 g	Protein	149 mg	Sodium
5 g	Fat	105 mg	Cholesterol

Chicken and Dumplings

Serves 6.

2½-3	pounds chicken parts
2	tablespoons whole wheat flour
2	tablespoons olive oil
½	teaspoon no-salt seasoning
1	large onion, chopped
1	teaspoon paprika
½	teaspoon powdered ginger
2½	cups boiling water

Remove the skin and all visible fat from the chicken. Wash under cold running water and dry well. Put the flour into a plastic or brown paper bag, add the chicken parts, one or two at a time, and shake to coat. Heat the oil in a Dutch oven. Add the chicken and brown on both sides, sprinkling with the no-salt seasoning as it browns. Sprinkle with the onion, paprika, and ginger. Add the boiling water and return to the boil. Cover tightly, reduce heat to low, and simmer for 45 to 55 minutes. While the stew is simmering, get the dumplings ready.

Dumplings

1	cup flour
1	tablespoon baking powder
½	teaspoon no-salt seasoning
1½	tablespoons safflower or canola oil
⅔	cup skim milk

Sift together the first three ingredients. Combine the oil and milk. Add to the dry ingredients and mix only until the flour is absorbed. Drop by large spoonfuls over the simmering stew. (Should make 6 dumplings.) Cover tightly, and simmer for an additional 15 minutes.

Serve at once.

Each serving provides:			
296	Calories	22 g	Carbohydrate
25 g	Protein	305 mg	Sodium
11 g	Fat	70 mg	Cholesterol

Great Chili

If you thought you'd never enjoy another bowl of steaming hot chili because of a cholesterol problem, think again! The following chili tastes just as good as the last good bowl of chili you remember. Maybe better.

Serves 6 to 8.

2	tablespoons olive oil
2	large (1 to 1½ pounds) whole chicken breasts, boned, skinned, and diced
3	cups tomato juice
2	cups onion, diced
½	cup celery, diced
½	cup green pepper, diced
2	apples, cored and sliced (but not peeled)
2	tablespoons chili powder
1	teaspoon no-salt seasoning
½	teaspoon garlic powder (or 1 small clove, minced)
½	teaspoon cumin
1	teaspoon basil
3-5	drops Tabasco sauce
2	cans (14 oz. each) kidney beans, undrained

In a Dutch oven, heat the oil and brown the chicken slightly. Add all of the remaining ingredients except the kidney beans and simmer for 1 hour. Add the kidney beans and simmer for an additional hour, or until the chili reaches the desired thickness.

Each serving provides:

288	Calories	33 g	Carbohydrate
27 g	Protein	857 mg	Sodium
6 g	Fat	49 mg	Cholesterol

Norma Rae's Chicken Fricassee

Serves 4.

2	tablespoons soft margarine
2½-3	pounds chicken parts
	Lemon pepper
1	cup chopped celery (including tops)
1	cup chopped green onions (including tops)

Melt the margarine in an electric frying pan or a skillet with a heavy lid and brown the chicken (skin on), sprinkling well with the lemon pepper as it browns. Drain the fat, but don't wipe the pan — you don't want to remove the flavor. Sprinkle the top of the chicken with the celery and green onions. Add a little bit of water (about ¼ cup) to the bottom of the pan. (The trick is not to put too much water in the pan, just enough to steam the chicken.) Cover tightly. Turn heat to high for 1 minute to start the chicken "steaming," then turn heat to low and simmer slowly for about 30 to 35 minutes, or until the chicken is tender. Remove the skin before eating.

Serve over rice.

Each serving provides:

361	Calories	2 g	Carbohydrate
33 g	Protein	200 mg	Sodium
24 g	Fat*	108 mg	Cholesterol

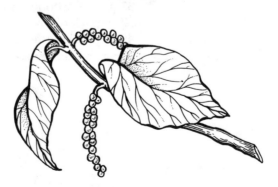

*Although this is mostly the "good" type of fat, you may want to save this recipe for a special occasion.

Chicken Creole

Serves 4.

2½-3   pounds chicken parts, skinned
2   tablespoons olive oil
2   tablespoons flour
2½   cups homemade chicken stock (or 2 10 oz. cans low-sodium
        chicken broth)
1   small onion, chopped
2   tablespoons green pepper, chopped
1   small can (5½ oz.) tomato paste
3   teaspoons lemon juice
2   teaspoons horseradish
½   teaspoon no-salt seasoning
½   teaspoon sugar
½   teaspoon thyme
¼   teaspoon Tabasco sauce
¼   teaspoon freshly ground black pepper
10   oz. fresh or frozen okra (if frozen, thawed and separated)

In an electric frying pan or Dutch oven, brown the chicken in the oil. Remove to a plate and turn heat off. Make a paste of the flour and 2 or 3 tablespoons of the chicken broth. Add to the pan with the rest of the chicken broth. Stir in all of the remaining ingredients (except the chicken and okra) and bring to a boil. Cook until the mixture thickens slightly. Add the chicken and the okra, spooning some of the sauce over the chicken. Cover and simmer for 40 minutes, or until the chicken is tender.

Serve over rice.

Each serving provides:			
360	Calories	18 g	Carbohydrate
42 g	Protein	1,319 mg	Sodium
13 g	Fat	106 mg	Cholesterol

Chicken Country Captain

You can make this ahead, refrigerate, and reheat at serving time. Traditionally, each portion of this dish is accompanied by a piece of crisp bacon, but you won't miss this a bit!

Serves 4.

3	pounds chicken, cut into pieces
¼	cup flour
1	teaspoon no-salt seasoning
½	teaspoon freshly ground pepper
2	tablespoons olive oil
1	tablespoon soft margarine
1	large onion, sliced
1	green pepper, seeded and chopped
1	clove garlic, minced
1½	teaspoons curry powder
¼	teaspoon thyme
¼	teaspoon nutmeg
1	can (28 oz.) stewed tomatoes, broken up with a fork
1	tablespoon fresh parsley, chopped
3	tablespoons black currants (or ½ cup raisins)
4	cups cooked rice
½	cup toasted slivered almonds (optional)

Skin the chicken and remove all visible fat. Make sure the drumsticks are separated from the thighs. Combine the flour, no-salt seasoning, and pepper. Dredge the chicken lightly in the seasoned flour. In a large skillet over medium-high heat, heat the oil and margarine. Brown the chicken pieces on all sides. Remove from the skillet and set aside. Add the onion, green pepper, garlic, curry powder, thyme, and nutmeg. Sauté until the vegetables are just tender. Stir in the tomatoes and parsley. Return the chicken to the skillet. Cover and simmer until the chicken is tender (about 25 minutes). Add the currants and simmer for an additional 5 minutes.

Arrange cooked rice in a circle on a heated platter. Place the chicken in the center and pour the sauce over all. If you like, garnish with the toasted almonds.

Each serving provides:			
666	Calories	86 g	Carbohydrate
44 g	Protein	675 mg	Sodium
16 g	Fat	114 mg	Cholesterol

Indian Curry Dinner

Serves 6 to 8.

4	whole chicken breasts, boned, skinned, and halved
¼	cup flour
2	tablespoons soft margarine
1	medium onion, chopped
1	apple, chopped but unpeeled
1½	cups chicken stock
3	tablespoons orange marmalade
1½	tablespoons curry powder
⅛	teaspoon cinnamon
1	small clove garlic, minced (or ⅛ teaspoon garlic powder)
1	tablespoon preserved ginger, chopped (or ½ teaspoon powdered ginger)
2	teaspoons cornstarch mixed with ¼ cup white wine

Dust the chicken breasts with the flour. In a large skillet or electric frying pan, brown the chicken in the margarine. Remove the chicken. Add all of the remaining ingredients to the skillet except the cornstarch and wine. Cover and cook until the apple is soft (about 5 minutes). Place the chicken in the sauce, turning to coat with the sauce, cover, and simmer slowly for about 5 to 10 minutes. (The chicken will be almost cooked after browning.) Remove the cover and stir in the wine and cornstarch. Bring to a boil and cook until thickened (about 2 to 3 minutes).

Serve with hot cooked rice and sprinkle with some or all of the following condiments: coarsely chopped peanuts, diced bananas sprinkled with lemon juice, and chopped ripe tomatoes.

Each serving provides:			
205	Calories	10 g	Carbohydrate
28 g	Protein	127 mg	Sodium
5 g	Fat	68 mg	Cholesterol

Lise's Chicken Tenders

Serves 4 to 6.

Chicken tenders are the finger-sized muscle on the back of each breast half. Most supermarkets carry them in their poultry department. If you are unable to find them, use chicken breast meat, cut into finger-sized portions.

	No-stick vegetable oil spray
2	pounds chicken tenders
½	cup onion, chopped
¾	cup fresh mushrooms, sliced
1¾	cups chicken stock
½	teaspoon no-salt seasoning
½	teaspoon oregano
1½	teaspoons Worcestershire sauce
1	teaspoon nutmeg
1	teaspoon paprika
¼	cup dry sherry
½	cup low-fat sour cream

Spray a Teflon frying pan with no-stick vegetable oil spray and brown the chicken. Remove from the pan. Sauté the onion until soft, then add all of the remaining ingredients except the sour cream and simmer very gently until the chicken is tender. Remove from heat and stir in the low-fat sour cream. Serve at once over hot noodles (about 1 cup, cooked, per person).

Each serving provides:

226	Calories	5 g	Carbohydrate
37 g	Protein	146 mg	Sodium
4 g	Fat	93 mg	Cholesterol

Ethel's Sweet and Sour Chicken Patties

This recipe comes from our good friend, Dr. Ethel Marliss, a radio commentator and food columnist. It's a wonderful "emergency" dish since the patties can be made ahead of time and frozen. Making the sauce is a relatively simple matter and can be done whenever you decide to serve the patties. Some steamed rice and a tossed green salad would make this meal suitable for family or very important guests!

Serves 4 to 6.

1	pound ground raw chicken (all white meat is best since it's lowest in fat)
⅔	cup celery, finely chopped
1	tablespoon low-sodium soy sauce
1	tablespoon dry sherry
1	green onion, finely chopped
2	cloves garlic, minced
1	teaspoon grated fresh ginger or ¼ teaspoon ground ginger
2	teaspoons cornstarch
¼	cup fine bread crumbs
3-4	tablespoons bread crumbs seasoned with no-salt seasoning and pepper
2	teaspoons safflower or canola oil

Combine all of the above ingredients except the additional breadcrumbs and oil) and shape into elongated oval patties (much nicer than round ones). The mixture will be quite soft, so it's best to wet your hands with a little cold water. Roll the patties in the seasoned breadcrumbs. Place the oil in a Teflon skillet and brown the patties lightly (about 2 to 3 minutes on each side). Remove from skillet. If you make the patties ahead and freeze, thaw before heating them in the Sweet and Sour Sauce below.

Sweet and Sour Sauce

2	teaspoons canola or safflower oil
1	green pepper, seeded and cut into strips
2	stalks celery, sliced diagonally
2	carrots, sliced diagonally
⅓	cup apple or pineapple juice
1	tablespoon low-sodium soy sauce
1	clove garlic, minced
	Pinch of ground ginger
3	tablespoons ketchup
4	teaspoons lemon juice or vinegar

In the same pan in which you cooked the chicken, heat the oil and sauté the green pepper, celery, and carrots until softened. Stir together the juice, soy sauce, garlic, ginger, ketchup, and lemon juice and add to the skillet. Bring to a boil, reduce heat, and carefully add the chicken patties. Simmer the patties in the sauce for about 20 minutes.

Each serving provides:

288	Calories	23 g	Carbohydrate
19 g	Protein	573 mg	Sodium
12 g	Fat	76 mg	Cholesterol

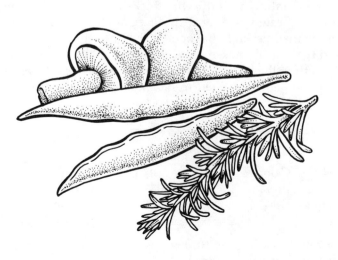

Paprika Chicken

This dish becomes extra special when served with homemade noodles. If you're not into making your own, fresh noodles can be purchased at a local delicatessen.

Serves 4.

3   tablespoons olive oil
1   large onion, chopped
2   tablespoons Hungarian paprika
5   tablespoons water
2½-3   pounds chicken parts, skin and all visible fat removed
       No-salt seasoning
       Freshly ground black pepper
2   medium tomatoes, chopped
1   large green pepper, seeded and chopped
¼   cup cold water
2   tablespoons flour
½   cup low-fat yogurt

Heat the olive oil in a 12-inch skillet (or electric frying pan). Add the onion and sauté until the onion is translucent. Stir in 1 tablespoon of the paprika. Add 3 tablespoons water and cook until most of the water evaporates. Add the chicken and sprinkle with the no-salt seasoning and freshly ground pepper. Add 2 tablespoons water. Cover tightly and cook over low heat for 20 minutes. Add the tomatoes and green pepper. Sprinkle with a little more no-salt seasoning and black pepper. Cover and cook for an additional 20 minutes, or until the chicken is tender. Remove the chicken to a heated serving dish. Place ¼ cup cold water and the flour in a small jar and shake well. Stir into the sauce left in the pan and cook until thickened, about 4 to 5 minutes. Remove from heat and stir in the yogurt, to which you have added the remaining 1 tablespoon paprika. When well blended, pour over the chicken. Serve over hot noodles.

Each serving provides:			
341	Calories	14 g	Carbohydrate
36 g	Protein	143 mg	Sodium
16 g	Fat*	107 mg	Cholesterol

*We know this looks high in fat, but it's actually a lower-fat version than the original — save it for special occasions.

5

Especially for the Microwave

MICROWAVE CHICKEN TIPS

Cooking chicken in the microwave is convenient, but the correct timing is very important, particularly for breasts. The trick to evenly cooked chicken is to elevate the breasts off the flat cooking container. A meat rack that is microwave safe is best for this, but you may also use chopsticks, evenly spaced in your baking dish, to elevate the chicken slightly. The outside edges of the chicken will cook faster than the centers, so halfway through cooking, turn the chicken over so that the pink side faces the outside of the dish, and the cooked outside edge faces the center. The chicken should be covered with wax paper; this sits loosely on top and allows much of the excess steam to escape while preventing spattering.

Here are some approximate cooking times for a 700-watt micro-wave oven:

- Chicken breasts: 4 half breasts, on a meat rack and covered with wax paper, will take 6 to 9 minutes (depending on their size) on full power.
- Chicken pieces: 2½ to 3 pounds, on a meat rack and covered with wax paper, will take 12 to 14 minutes on full power. If the chicken is in a sauce, it will take much longer (20 to 25 minutes).
- Rock Cornish game hens: 6 to 7 minutes per pound (elevate the bottom of the bird).

As a rule of thumb, cook chicken in the microwave for 7 minutes per pound.

Chicken and Broccoli Pasta

Serves 4 to 6.

2-3	cups uncooked fusilli (spiral-shaped) pasta
2	tablespoons lemon juice
2	cups fresh, chopped (or frozen) broccoli
⅓	cup onion, chopped
2	cloves garlic, minced
1	sweet red pepper, cut into long strips
2	tablespoons water
2	cups cooked chicken, chopped
1	teaspoon oregano
1	teaspoon basil
¼	teaspoon black pepper
1	cup low-fat yogurt
2	tablespoons Parmesan cheese

Prepare the fusilli as directed on the package but add 2 tablespoons lemon juice to water called for on the package. Drain the cooked pasta and set aside. In a 2-quart casserole dish, combine the broccoli, onion, garlic, red pepper, and 2 tablespoons water. Cover and microwave on high for 4 to 6 minutes, or until the vegetables are tender-crisp, stirring once. Stir in the fusilli, chicken, oregano, basil, and black pepper. Cover and microwave on high for an additional 3 to 6 minutes, or until well heated through, stirring once. Blend in the yogurt and Parmesan cheese.

Each serving provides:

321	Calories	39 g	Carbohydrate
26 g	Protein	131 mg	Sodium
6 g	Fat	54 mg	Cholesterol

Bill's Favorite Chicken

Serves 4.

2½-3 pounds chicken pieces
3   green onions, sliced
½   green pepper, seeded and diced
1   tablespoon olive oil
1   can (7½ oz.) tomato sauce with onions
1   tablespoon dry mustard
½   teaspoon Worcestershire sauce
2   tablespoons vinegar
2   tablespoons low-sodium soy sauce
1   tablespoon brown sugar

Skin the chicken pieces, wash them under cold water, and pat dry with paper towels. Place the chicken in a shallow baking dish. Sauté the green onions and green pepper in the olive oil. Add the tomato sauce, mustard, Worcestershire sauce, vinegar, soy sauce, and brown sugar. Bring to a boil, then remove from heat. Pour the sauce over the chicken. Cover with wax paper and cook on full power for 15 to 20 minutes, turning the chicken and rotating the dish after 10 minutes. Let stand for 10 minutes (the chicken will continue to cook). Serve over hot spaghetti.

Each serving provides:			
260	Calories	11 g	Carbohydrate
34 g	Protein	738 mg	Sodium
9 g	Fat	105 mg	Cholesterol

Bea's Chicken Cacciatore

Chicken Cacciatore has sometimes been referred to as the Coq au Vin of Italy. It loses none of its robust flavor by being cooked in the microwave.

Serves 3 to 4.

2	pounds chicken breasts and drumsticks, skinned
	No-stick vegetable oil spray
2	cloves garlic, minced
1	medium onion, coarsely chopped
½	cup green pepper, diced
1	can (19 oz.) tomatoes, drained and broken up with a fork
1	can (5½ oz.) low-salt tomato paste
½	teaspoon thyme
½	teaspoon allspice
1	bay leaf
½	teaspoon black pepper
½	cup dry red wine (optional)

Brown the chicken in a Teflon pan that has been sprayed with no-stick vegetable oil spray. Add the garlic and cook 1 minute. Add the onion and green pepper and cook for an additional 1 minute. Combine all of the remaining ingredients in a 2-quart casserole dish, cover, and microwave on high for 5 minutes, stirring halfway through cooking. Add the browned chicken, garlic, onion, and pepper to the casserole dish and cover well with the sauce. Cook on medium heat for 15 minutes, stirring and turning every 5 minutes. Serve over hot pasta.

Each serving provides:

226	Calories	16 g	Carbohydrate
32 g	Protein	345 mg	Sodium
4 g	Fat	87 mg	Cholesterol

Chicken Miriam

Serves 4 to 6.

1	cup low-fat yogurt
2	tablespoons freshly grated ginger
2	cloves garlic, minced
¼	teaspoon ground cardamom
½	teaspoon chili powder
½	teaspoon cinnamon
2½-3	pounds chicken, cut into pieces and skinned

Combine all of the ingredients except the chicken pieces. Pour this yogurt sauce over the chicken, mixing well and let it marinate in the refrigerator all day or overnight.

Place the chicken in a baking dish, cover with wax paper, and cook on full power for 15 minutes. Rearrange the chicken pieces and baste with the pan juices. Cook for another 3 to 5 minutes on full power, covered with wax paper.

Each serving provides:

176	Calories	4 g	Carbohydrate
28 g	Protein	127 mg	Sodium
4 g	Fat	87 mg	Cholesterol

Pineapple Chicken

Serves 4.

2½-3	pounds chicken, cut into pieces and skinned
2-3	tablespoons flour
½-1	teaspoon no-salt seasoning
½	teaspoon pepper
1	cup pineapple chunks*
⅔	cup pineapple juice (or ⅔ cup juice from pineapple chunks)
¼	cup brown sugar
1	tablespoon cornstarch
1	tablespoon apple cider vinegar
3	tablespoons ketchup
½	cup water
	Paprika

Dredge the chicken pieces in the flour seasoned with the no-salt seasoning and pepper, and spread in a baking pan. Combine the pineapple with the juice and pour over the chicken. Cover with wax paper and cook on full power for 15 minutes. Rearrange the chicken pieces. Combine the brown sugar, cornstarch, vinegar, ketchup, and water in a small bowl. Heat on full power 3 to 4 minutes to thicken. Pour over the chicken. Sprinkle with the paprika. Cover with wax paper and cook for another 3 to 5 minutes on full power.

*Or use the recipe for Zucchini Pineapple on page 260.

Each serving provides:			
327	Calories	37 g	Carbohydrate
33 g	Protein	256 mg	Sodium
5 g	Fat	105 mg	Cholesterol

Nell's Curried Chicken

A true curry dish contains a blend of spices. This microwave dish uses six spices, so we think it's not only delicious, but authentic as well!

Serves 4.

1	cup chicken stock, preferably homemade
1	onion, thinly sliced
1	clove garlic, minced
1	apple, peeled and diced
½	cup raisins
½	teaspoon ginger
½	teaspoon turmeric
½	teaspoon chili powder
½	teaspoon coriander
¼	teaspoon cayenne pepper
¼	teaspoon cinnamon
4	half chicken breasts, skinned, boned, and diced

Combine ½ cup of the stock and the onion and garlic in a 2-quart casserole dish. Microwave on high for 3 minutes. Stir in the apple, raisins, and spices. Add the chicken and the remaining stock. Cover with plastic wrap or wax paper but turn back 1 corner to allow steam to escape. Cook on medium heat for 15 minutes.

Serve over cooked rice.

Each serving provides:

222	Calories	22 g	Carbohydrate
29 g	Protein	96 mg	Sodium
2 g	Fat	68 mg	Cholesterol

Microwave Chicken Curry

You'll never miss the demon salt in this fiery dish. It's hot!

Serves 6.

1	tablespoon soft margarine
1	medium onion, chopped
1	medium green pepper, chopped
2	cloves garlic, minced
2	medium tomatoes, peeled and thinly sliced
1	medium apple, peeled, and chopped
¼	cup flour
1	tablespoon curry powder
1	tablespoon ground allspice
1	teaspoon ground ginger
½	teaspoon black pepper
2½-3	pounds chicken, cut into pieces with skin and all visible fat removed
1½	cups hot water
1	teaspoon low-salt chicken bouillon mix

Melt the margarine in a large (3 to 5 quarts) casserole dish. Stir in the onion, green pepper, and garlic, and microwave on high for 3 to 5 minutes, or until the onion and green pepper are soft. Stir once during cooking. Add the tomatoes and apple.

Mix the flour, curry powder, allspice, ginger, and pepper. Stir the flour mixture into the vegetables. Add the chicken, hot water, and bouillon mix. Microwave on medium-high power until the chicken next to the bone is no longer pink and the sauce has thickened. This will take 25 to 30 minutes. Stir twice during cooking.

Serve with the following condiments and hot, fluffy rice: chopped bananas, chopped green onions, and plumped raisins. (To plump the raisins, soak them in hot water for 5 to 10 minutes.)

Each serving provides:			
193	Calories	13 g	Carbohydrate
23 g	Protein	109 mg	Sodium
5 g	Fat	70 mg	Cholesterol

Quick Fix Chicken

This might quite easily be the simplest, fastest recipe in the book. It was tested in a 700-watt microwave with a turntable. The breasts were roughly 8 oz. each and the timing was perfect.

Serves 4.

4   half chicken breasts, skinned
½   teaspoon oregano
1   clove garlic, minced
1   small can (7½ oz.) tomato sauce

Arrange the breasts in a glass 10-inch pie plate in a spoke-like fashion (the thickest parts of the breasts turned toward the rim). Stir the oregano and garlic into the tomato sauce and spoon over the chicken. Cover tightly with plastic wrap and prick a tiny hole in the center. Cook on high for *9 minutes.** Allow the dish to stand, covered, for 2 minutes.

This is wonderful with noodles, but may be served with rice as well. Some cooked mushrooms and a tossed green salad would make this a very satisfying meal.

*Remember, chicken on the bone takes longer in the microwave than boneless.

Each serving provides:			
147	Calories	4 g	Carbohydrate
28 g	Protein	398 mg	Sodium
2 g	Fat	68 mg	Cholesterol

6
Baked Chicken Entrées

As you'll soon notice, this is the largest section in the book. And for good reason. Chicken, with its tender, juicy texture, responds well to a variety of seasonings, flavorings, sauces, and special touches that are enhanced by oven cooking.

Many cooks appreciate oven-baked dishes simply because of the freedom they afford. Once the ingredients have been assembled, your trusty timer and preset temperature take over!

CHICKEN BREASTS

Chicken Baklava

The rich-tasting sauce, infused with the flavors of lemon and dill, complements the chicken, artichokes, and mushrooms wrapped in individual packets of flaky filo pastry. This dish will delight the palate of any gourmet. It's amazing that something this good is low in cholesterol.

Serves 12.

3	whole chicken breasts, skinned, boned, and halved
1	can (14 oz.) artichoke hearts, drained
1½	cups sliced wild mushrooms*
2	teaspoons safflower or canola oil
1	tablespoon fresh dill, chopped
9	sheets filo pastry**
5	tablespoons safflower or canola oil
5	tablespoons fine bread crumbs
	No-stick vegetable oil spray

To cook the chicken breasts, place in medium-sized saucepan and cover with water or chicken stock. Bring to a boil. Immediately reduce heat, cover, and simmer gently for 10 to 12 minutes. Remove from heat. Cut the chicken into bite-size pieces. Cut each artichoke heart into 6 to 8 pieces. Add to the chicken. Sauté mushrooms in the 2 teaspoons of oil. Add to the chicken and artichokes. (Save any juice for the following sauce.) Add the fresh dill to the chicken mixture. Mix with the sauce below.

Sauce

3	tablespoons soft margarine
3	tablespoons flour
1	can (14 oz.) low-fat evaporated milk
1½	teaspoons grated lemon rind
½	teaspoon lemon pepper
1	tablespoon fresh dill, chopped
	Juice from sautéed mushrooms (about 1 or 2 tablespoons)

*If wild mushrooms aren't available, cultivated shiitake or button mushrooms can be substituted.

**You'll have to purchase a full package, but filo pastry will keep up to two weeks in the refrigerator and up to two months in the freezer.

Melt the margarine in a small saucepan. Stir in the flour until absorbed. Gradually stir in the evaporated milk. Cook over medium heat, stirring constantly, until thickened (like a fairly thick cream sauce). Stir in the lemon rind, lemon pepper, dill, and juice from sautéed mushrooms. Stir into the chicken mixture. Let cool.

To assemble the baklava: Unroll the filo pastry carefully. Using a corner, count out 9 sheets. Keep the 9 sheets covered with a damp cloth. Lay 1 sheet of filo pastry down on your work surface and lightly brush with oil, making sure to brush right to the edges. Sprinkle with 1 tablespoon of the bread crumbs. Lay a second sheet directly over the first and again brush lightly with oil and sprinkle with crumbs. Lay a third sheet on top of the second and brush with oil but do not sprinkle with crumbs. Cut these layered sheets into 4 squares. Place roughly 2½ tablespoons of the chicken mixture in the center of each square and fold up like an envelope. (Or you can gather the edges of each square and bring them up to form a "pouch." Squeeze together at the top and the top edges will fan out a bit and stay that way during baking.) Repeat this process with remaining filo pastry sheets.

Place the chicken baklava on a baking sheet that has been sprayed with the no-stick vegetable oil spray and bake on the middle shelf of a preheated 375° oven for 25 minutes.

Note: These freeze very well. Freeze *before* baking. Let thaw at room temperature for 1 hour before baking. This is wonderful to have on hand for unexpected guests. Take out as many individual servings as required. Wild rice and fresh asparagus (or green beans) would make this a meal you would be proud to serve to anyone. A few very lightly sautéed cherry tomatoes and a tossed green salad would complete the meal.

Each serving provides:			
328	Calories	35 g	Carbohydrate
22 g	Protein	339 mg	Sodium
11 g	Fat	40 mg	Cholesterol

Bombay Chicken

Serves 8 to 10.

8-10   half chicken breasts, boned and skinned

Filling

2   tablespoons soft margarine
2   tablespoons olive oil
1   small onion, chopped
1   small apple, peeled and chopped
½   cup golden raisins
½   teaspoon ginger
2   teaspoons curry powder
½   teaspoon pepper
⅓   cup water chestnuts, finely chopped
1½   cups cooked rice
        Paprika

Heat the margarine and oil in a saucepan. Add the onion and apple and cook gently until tender. Remove from heat and add the raisins, spices, water chestnuts, and rice. Stir with a fork to mix.

Lay the chicken breasts flat between two pieces of plastic wrap and pound to twice their original size. Spoon the filling onto the breasts and fold the ends of each breast so the filling will not fall out. Place the breasts in a 9 × 13-inch baking pan. (Any extra filling can be spooned around the sides of the pan.) Sprinkle with a bit of paprika. Bake, covered, in a preheated 350° oven for 30 minutes. Uncover and bake an additional 15 minutes. Serve with the following sauce.

Sauce

2½   tablespoons flour
1½   cups skim milk
1   teaspoon no-salt seasoning
1   teaspoon dry sherry
½   teaspoon lemon pepper
1   teaspoon curry powder
¼   cup chutney (cut up any large pieces)*

Mix the flour with a little milk to make a paste. Add to the remaining milk and boil for 1 minute. Add the remaining ingredients. Stir to blend well. This makes a medium-thick sauce.

*Major Grey brand chutney is our favorite.

Each serving provides:

304	Calories	28 g	Carbohydrate
30 g	Protein	194 mg	Sodium
7 g	Fat	69 mg	Cholesterol

Asparagus-Stuffed Chicken Breasts in Filo Bon Bon

For holiday entertaining, what could be more attractive than these beautifully arranged chicken rolls designed to resemble a Christmas Bon Bon cracker? They would also be perfect for a special New Year's Eve dinner party.

Serves 8.

8   half chicken breasts, skinned and boned
8   cooked asparagus spears
6   sheets of filo pastry, thawed*
4   tablespoons safflower or canola oil
4   tablespoons bread crumbs
    No-stick vegetable oil spray

Pound the chicken breasts very slightly, just to an even thickness. Place an asparagus spear in the center of each breast and roll up.

Unroll the filo pastry carefully. Using a corner, count out 6 sheets. Keep the 6 sheets covered with a damp cloth. Lay 1 sheet of filo pastry down on a clean work surface and lightly brush with oil. Sprinkle with 1 tablespoon of the bread crumbs. Lay a second sheet directly on top of the first and again brush lightly with oil and sprinkle with bread crumbs. Lay a third sheet on top of the second but do not brush with oil or sprinkle with crumbs. Cut the layered pastry into 4 squares. Place an asparagus-filled chicken breast horizontally across each square and roll up. Twist each end and place on a cookie sheet that has been sprayed with a no-stick vegetable oil spray. Repeat with the remaining filo pastry and chicken breasts. Bake in a preheated 350° oven for 25 minutes. You can make these ahead of time and freeze but let them thaw to room temperature before baking. Serve with the following sauce.

*If you've purchased a full package for this recipe, note that the remaining pastry will keep about two weeks in the refrigerator and up to two months in the freezer.

Each serving of chicken provides:			
386	Calories	41 g	Carbohydrate
34 g	Protein	340 mg	Sodium
9 g	Fat	69 mg	Cholesterol

Pimiento Cream Sauce

2	tablespoons soft margarine
2	tablespoons flour
2	cups skim milk (or low-fat evaporated milk)
½	teaspoon no-salt seasoning
	Pinch of nutmeg
1	teaspoon dill
½	teaspoon lemon pepper
3	tablespoons pimiento, coarsely chopped

Melt the margarine in a small saucepan over medium heat. Stir in the flour until absorbed. Slowly stir in the milk. Cook over medium heat until slightly thickened. Stir in all remaining ingredients, then serve on the side with the Asparagus-Stuffed Chicken Breasts.

Each serving of pimiento cream sauce provides:

56	Calories	5 g	Carbohydrate
2 g	Protein	122 mg	Sodium
3 g	Fat	1 mg	Cholesterol

Baked Apple Chicken Breasts

Serves 6.

6	half chicken breasts, bone in but skinned
4	tablespoons flour
½	teaspoon lemon pepper
2	tablespoons olive oil
2	cloves garlic, lightly crushed
3	apples, cored and quartered
2	tablespoons brown sugar
1½	cups unsweetened apple juice
½	cup dry sherry (or water)
½	teaspoon ginger
2	tablespoons cornstarch
¼	cup cold water

Dredge the chicken in the flour mixed with the lemon pepper. Heat the oil in a skillet and brown the chicken along with the garlic. Remove the chicken and discard the garlic. Add the apples to the skillet and sprinkle with the brown sugar. Brown the apples. Place the chicken and apples in a casserole dish and pour the apple juice and sherry on top. Sprinkle with the ginger. Cover and bake for 30 minutes in a preheated 350° oven. Remove the chicken and apples from the sauce and keep warm. Pour the sauce into a small saucepan. Dissolve the cornstarch in the water and stir into the sauce. Bring to a boil and cook, stirring constantly, until thickened. Pour over the chicken and apples and serve.

Each serving provides:			
298	Calories	31 g	Carbohydrate
28 g	Protein	149 mg	Sodium
6 g	Fat	68 mg	Cholesterol

Brent's Favorite Chicken Breasts

A wonderful, tender chicken dish that's perfect for company because it can be partially prepared the night before and made oven-ready early in the day. It uses lots of bread crumbs, so you may want to skip the rolls!

Serves 8.

8	half chicken breasts, boned and skinned
2	cups buttermilk
	Juice of 1 lemon
½	teaspoon Worcestershire sauce
½	teaspoon celery seed
¾	teaspoon paprika
2	cloves garlic, crushed
3	cups fine bread crumbs
	No-stick vegetable oil spray

The day before serving, cut each chicken half breast in half (for 16 pieces). Combine the buttermilk, lemon juice, Worcestershire sauce, celery seed, paprika, and garlic in a large bowl. Add the chicken pieces to the mixture, coating each piece well, and marinate in the bowl, covered, in the refrigerator. The next morning, remove the chicken, one piece at a time, leaving a good coating of buttermilk on each. Coat well with the bread crumbs. Arrange on a shallow pan or cookie sheet that has been sprayed with a no-stick vegetable oil spray. Cover and refrigerate until ready to bake. Uncover and bake in a preheated 350° oven for 35 to 40 minutes.

Note: If you're making your own bread crumbs, 1 slice stale bread equals ½ cup crumbs.

	Each serving provides:		
299	Calories	30 g	Carbohydrate
34 g	Protein	404 mg	Sodium
4 g	Fat	72 mg	Cholesterol

Cacciatore Style Chicken Breasts

Serves 6.

3   whole chicken breasts, skinned, boned, and halved
½   teaspoon no-salt seasoning
        Freshly ground black pepper to taste
1   medium onion, chopped
½   medium green pepper, chopped
2   tablespoons olive oil
½   cup mild red chili sauce
2   tablespoons white wine (or water)
1   teaspoon Worcestershire sauce
1   teaspoon brown sugar

Cut away any membrane or fat on the chicken breasts. Place the pieces of chicken side by side in a shallow baking dish. Sprinkle with the no-salt seasoning and freshly ground black pepper.

In a medium-sized Teflon skillet, sauté the onion and green pepper in the olive oil until tender. Stir in the chili sauce, white wine, Worcestershire sauce, and brown sugar. Spoon this sauce over the breasts and bake in a preheated 350° oven for 30 to 40 minutes, or until breasts are cooked through.

Each serving provides:			
204	Calories	8 g	Carbohydrate
28 g	Protein	391 mg	Sodium
6 g	Fat	68 mg	Cholesterol

Chicken Breasts with Cranberries and Oranges

Great holiday fare for the dedicated cholesterol counter.

Serves 3 to 4.

4	half chicken breasts, skinned and boned
¼	cup chicken stock
	Orange rind from 1 orange, plus juice
1	teaspoon thyme
1	tablespoon cornstarch
¾	cup jellied cranberry sauce

Lay the chicken breasts in the bottom of a flat casserole. Combine the chicken stock, orange rind, and thyme and pour over the breasts. Cover and bake for 20 minutes in a preheated 350° oven. Remove the casserole from the oven. Combine the cornstarch and orange juice, stirring until smooth. Add the cranberry sauce. Carefully pour any accumulated juices from the casserole into the cranberry mixture. Heat this sauce 3 to 5 minutes in a saucepan or 1½ to 2 minutes on high in the microwave until thickened. Pour over the chicken breasts in the casserole and return to the oven to bake, uncovered, for an additional 20 to 25 minutes.

Each serving provides:			
232	Calories	25 g	Carbohydrate
28 g	Protein	96 mg	Sodium
2 g	Fat	68 mg	Cholesterol

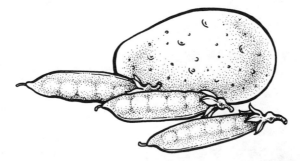

Quick Cranberry and Orange-Glazed Chicken Breasts for a Crowd

This recipe doubles easily.

Serves 8 to 10.

8   oz. jar currant jelly
4   tablespoons frozen orange juice concentrate
1   can (14 oz.) jellied cranberry sauce
1   teaspoon grated orange rind
8-10 half chicken breasts (or chicken parts)

Place all the ingredients except the chicken in a small saucepan. Heat gently until the jelly is melted and the ingredients are well blended. Brush on the chicken breasts and bake in a preheated 350° oven. Brush with the sauce several times while baking. Boneless breasts will take 30 to 35 minutes. Breasts on the bone will take 45 minutes. If using dark and white meat parts, remove the breasts when done and leave the dark meat in for 60 minutes, or until done.

Note: Line the baking pan with foil before baking and use the top third of the oven since a sweet glaze like this has a tendency to burn.

Each serving provides:			
278	Calories	38 g	Carbohydrate
28 g	Protein	94 mg	Sodium
2 g	Fat	68 mg	Cholesterol

Chicken Breasts in Maple Syrup

An easily prepared dinner for two. Steamed carrots and broccoli would round out the flavor and add color to this meal.

Serves 2.

2	tablespoons flour
¼	teaspoon paprika
½	teaspoon black pepper
2	half chicken breasts, bone in but skinned
	No-stick vegetable oil spray
1	tablespoon soft margarine
1	medium onion, thinly sliced and pushed into rings
2	tablespoons maple syrup
3	tablespoons hot water

Place the flour, paprika, and black pepper in a small paper bag. Shake the chicken breasts, one at a time, in the flour mixture. Spray a small skillet well with no-stick vegetable oil spray and sauté the breasts until golden brown on both sides. Remove to a shallow casserole dish. Melt the margarine in the same skillet and sauté the onion rings until they are soft and lightly colored. Spoon the cooked onions over the chicken breasts and drizzle with the maple syrup, one tablespoon per breast. Add the hot water to the skillet and let it boil up, scraping the skillet as the liquid boils. Spoon this around the bottom of the baking dish. Cover and bake in a preheated 350° oven for 25 to 30 minutes. (Small breasts take 25 minutes and larger ones about 30 minutes.) Don't overcook or the breasts will dry out.

Each serving provides:			
278	Calories	22 g	Carbohydrate
29 g	Protein	156 mg	Sodium
8 g	Fat	68 mg	Cholesterol

Crunchy Apricot-Stuffed Chicken Breasts

This was a very popular dish at one of our many recipe-testing parties. We gathered all of our friends with high cholesterol for these testings — eventually the parties became so popular that some people were claiming to have a cholesterol problem just to get on the guest list.

Serves 12.

12   half chicken breasts, boned and skinned
      Lemon pepper
12   dried apricot halves

Stuffing

2½   cups soft (freshly made) bread crumbs
10   dried apricots, cut into slivers (about ½ cup)
1   medium onion, chopped
¼   cup raisins
½   cup water chestnuts, cut into quarters
½   teaspoon powdered sage
¼   teaspoon black pepper
4   tablespoons orange juice

Remove all visible fat from the breasts and place one piece at a time between two pieces of plastic wrap. Flatten each breast with a mallet to twice its original size. Mix all stuffing ingredients together until well blended. Place two tablespoons of the stuffing in the center of each breast, fold the ends over, and roll up. Place the breasts in a single layer in a large baking dish, sprinkle with the lemon pepper, and place a dried apricot half on top of each breast. Cover with foil and bake in a slow (250°) oven for 1½ hours. Serve with the following sauce.

Sauce

2   tablespoons soft margarine
2   tablespoons flour
1   cup apricot nectar
½   cup orange juice
¼   cup white wine
1½   teaspoons grated orange rind
½   teaspoon salt or no-salt seasoning
¼   teaspoon black pepper
¼   teaspoon sage

Melt the margarine in a small saucepan. Stir in the flour and, when well blended, gradually stir in the remaining ingredients in the order listed. Bring to a boil, stirring constantly. Reduce heat and simmer, stirring constantly, until the sauce has thickened.

	Each serving provides:		
232	Calories	19 g	Carbohydrate
29 g	Protein	276 mg	Sodium
4 g	Fat	69 mg	Cholesterol

Stuffed Chicken Breasts in Filo Pastry with Piquant Cranberry Sauce

Serves 8.

	No-stick vegetable oil spray
¾	cup green onion, chopped
¾	cup celery, chopped
½	teaspoon dried thyme
8	half chicken breasts, skinned and boned
6	sheets of filo pastry, thawed
4	tablespoons safflower oil
4	tablespoons bread crumbs

Spray a medium-sized skillet well with no-stick vegetable oil spray and sauté the green onion and celery until soft. Stir in the thyme. Cool.

Pound the chicken breasts slightly, just to an even thickness (about ⅓ inch). Place about 1 tablespoon of the sautéed vegetables in the center of each breast and wrap the chicken to enclose it.

Unroll the filo pastry carefully. Using a corner, count out 6 sheets. (Return any remaining pastry to the refrigerator and use within 10 to 14 days.) Keep the 6 sheets covered with a damp cloth. Lay 1 sheet of filo pastry down on your work surface and lightly brush with oil. Sprinkle with 1 tablespoon of bread crumbs. Lay a second sheet directly over the first and again brush with oil and sprinkle with crumbs. Lay a third sheet on top of the second and brush with oil but don't sprinkle with crumbs. Cut these layered sheets into 4 squares. Place a stuffed chicken breast in the center of each square and fold up like an envelope. (Or you can gather the edges of each square of filo pastry and bring them up to form a "pouch." Squeeze together just at the top and the edges will fan out a bit and stay that way during baking.) Place the chicken packages on a baking sheet that has been sprayed with the no-stick vegetable oil spray and bake in a preheated 350° oven for 25 minutes. Serve with the following sauce.

Each serving of chicken provides:			
389	Calories	41 g	Carbohydrate
34 g	Protein	350 mg	Sodium
9 g	Fat	69 mg	Cholesterol

Piquant Cranberry Sauce

7   oz. jellied cranberry sauce
⅓   cup mild, red chili sauce
¼   cup white wine vinegar

Place the sauce ingredients in a small saucepan and stir over medium heat until the jelly has melted. Serve warm.

Each serving of piquant cranberry sauce provides:

50	Calories	13 g	Carbohydrate
0 g	Protein	158 mg	Sodium
0 g	Fat	0 mg	Cholesterol

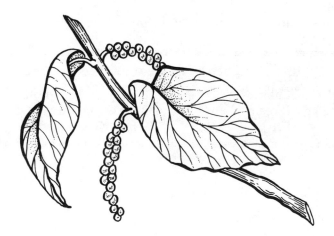

Lemon-Mustard Chicken Breasts

These breasts have a wonderful lemony mustard flavor. If you're on a salt-restricted diet, substitute low-sodium for the Dijon mustard. Don't overcook the chicken or it will be a little dry.

Serves 6.

½ cup fine bread crumbs
2 teaspoons fresh lemon rind, grated
½ teaspoon lemon pepper
3 tablespoons Dijon mustard
3 tablespoons fresh lemon juice
1 tablespoon lime juice
3 whole chicken breasts, skinned, boned, and halved
   No-stick vegetable oil spray

Combine the bread crumbs, lemon rind, and lemon pepper and spread onto a flat dish. Combine the mustard, lemon juice, and lime juice. Dip the chicken breasts in the lemon-mustard mixture, then in the bread crumb mixture and place in a 9 × 13-inch pan that has been sprayed with a no-stick vegetable oil spray. Bake in a preheated 375° oven for 15 minutes on each side, or until chicken is done.

Garnish with fresh parsley and lemon slices.

	Each serving provides:		
176	Calories	8 g	Carbohydrate
28 g	Protein	430 mg	Sodium
2 g	Fat	69 mg	Cholesterol

Quick Lemon-Mustard Chicken Breasts

Serves 6.

⅓   cup lemon marmalade
2   tablespoons Dijon mustard*
6   half chicken breasts, skinned

Place the lemon marmalade and the Dijon mustard in a small saucepan. Heat gently until the marmalade has melted, stirring with a fork until well blended with the mustard. Brush 6 skinned half chicken breasts with this glaze and bake in a preheated 350° oven. Line the baking pan with foil before baking since this glaze has a tendency to burn (but the flavor is great!). Boneless breasts will take 30 to 35 minutes. Breasts with the bone in will take 45 minutes. (This glaze is also wonderful brushed on Rock Cornish game hens or small broilers.) Brush with the glaze several times while baking. If using on chicken parts, remove the breasts after 45 minutes (bone in) and leave the hind quarters in for 60 minutes.

*If you're on a salt-restricted diet, substitute a low-sodium mustard.

Each serving provides:			
181	Calories	13 g	Carbohydrate
27 g	Protein	229 mg	Sodium
2 g	Fat	68 mg	Cholesterol

Chicken Breasts Mandalay with Couscous

Serves 3 to 4.

4	half chicken breasts, bone in but skinned
3	tablespoons flour
1	tablespoon curry powder
1	teaspoon no-salt seasoning
2	tablespoons olive oil

Coat the chicken breasts in a mixture of the flour, curry powder, and no-salt seasoning. Heat the oil in a skillet. Brown the breasts on all sides and place in a baking dish. Cover with the following sauce.

Sauce

1	medium onion, chopped
1	tablespoon soft margarine
1	cup apricot puree*
½	teaspoon no-salt seasoning
1	tablespoon curry powder
4	teaspoons white wine vinegar
2	tablespoons honey

Sauté the onion in the margarine in a small saucepan until soft. Add all of the remaining ingredients. Bring to a boil and simmer for 5 minutes. Spoon over the chicken. Bake, covered, in a pre-heated 350° oven for 45 minutes, or until breasts are done. Delicious served with the following couscous (you can substitute rice if couscous isn't available).

*Puree fresh or canned apricots in the blender or food processor.

Couscous

3   cups water
1½   cups couscous
1½   tablespoons soft margarine

In a large saucepan over high heat, bring the water to a boil. Slowly stir in the couscous. Add the margarine. Remove from heat, cover, and let stand for 15 minutes. Fluff with a fork.

Each serving provides:

616	Calories	78 g	Carbohydrate
38 g	Protein	185 mg	Sodium
16 g	Fat	68 mg	Cholesterol

Simple Orange-Ginger Chicken Breasts

Serves 6.

3   whole chicken breasts, bone in but skinned and halved
6   tablespoons orange juice concentrate, thawed
6   teaspoons low-sodium soy sauce
2   teaspoons powdered ginger
      Paprika

Remove all visible fat from the chicken breasts. Combine the orange juice concentrate, soy sauce, and ginger. Place the chicken breasts in a shallow baking pan and spoon the sauce over the top. (Roll the chicken around a bit in the sauce.) Sprinkle with paprika and bake in a preheated 350° oven for 30 minutes, basting frequently.

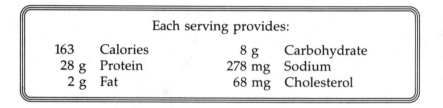

Each serving provides:

163	Calories	8 g	Carbohydrate
28 g	Protein	278 mg	Sodium
2 g	Fat	68 mg	Cholesterol

Oven-Fried Mustard-Caraway Chicken Breasts

Serves 12.

¼   cup mustard (preferably Dijon)*
⅓   cup low-fat yogurt
2-2½ cups fine rye bread crumbs
1½   teaspoons caraway seeds
6   whole chicken breasts, bone in but skinned and halved
        No-stick vegetable oil spray

Mix the mustard with the yogurt. In another bowl, toss together the bread crumbs and caraway seeds. Spread each piece of chicken with the mustard-yogurt mixture, then roll in the bread crumbs. Place the chicken in a single layer on a baking sheet that's been sprayed with no-stick vegetable oil spray. Spray the chicken with the oil as well — it will be nice and crisp after baking. Bake in a preheated 350° oven for 45 minutes. If you use boneless chicken breasts, reduce baking time to 30 minutes, but you'll find that the meat stays just a little more moist when cooked on the bone.

*Dijon mustard is high in sodium. If you're on a salt-restricted diet, substitute a low-sodium mustard.

Each serving provides:

163	Calories	6 g	Carbohydrate
28 g	Protein	283 mg	Sodium
2 g	Fat	69 mg	Cholesterol

Party Chicken Breasts

These can be prepared for baking early in the day. Baked rice and a crisp salad would be easy, last-minute accompaniments.

Serves 12.

6	whole chicken breasts, skinned, boned, and halved
3-4	tablespoons flour
¾	cup (6 oz.) low-fat yogurt
¼	teaspoon basil
¼	teaspoon thyme
1	tablespoon onion, grated
	Juice of 1 lemon
	Dash of salt and pepper
1	cup finely crushed cereal crumbs
½	cup grated low-fat cheddar cheese
	No-stick vegetable oil spray

Dust the chicken with the flour. Mix the yogurt, basil, thyme, grated onion, lemon juice, salt, and pepper. In a separate bowl, mix the cereal crumbs with the cheese. Dip the chicken in the yogurt mixture, then in the cereal crumbs. Place the chicken in a shallow baking dish that has been sprayed with no-stick vegetable oil spray. Tuck in the edges of the chicken to make mounds; the chicken looks more attractive and doesn't dry out while baking. Cover and bake in a preheated 350° oven for 30 minutes. Uncover and bake an additional 30 minutes.

Note: If you prepare this dish early in the day, do *not* cover the chicken until you are ready to bake it. Covering the chicken will result in soggy crumbs; uncovered, the crumbs stay dry.

Each serving provides:

210	Calories	14 g	Carbohydrate
31 g	Protein	248 mg	Sodium
3 g	Fat	73 mg	Cholesterol

Chicken Breast in a Paper Bag
for One or Two*

This is a perfect method for a hurry-up meal. Keep a supply of paper lunch bags on hand — you'll enjoy this neat way of baking single portions of chicken. The bag seals in the flavor while helping to keep the chicken moist — but don't overcook it.

Boneless Breast

There are several variations.

1. Sprinkle a half breast, boned and skinned, with tarragon, paprika, and parsley flakes. Place in small paper lunch bag. Fold the end to seal. Place on a cookie sheet and bake in a preheated 425° oven for 15 minutes.

2. Same method as above but instead of the herbs and spices, mix a bit of mustard (to taste) into a tablespoon of honey and smear over the breast. Generously cover the breast with chopped chives before placing in the bag.

3. Spray the breast lightly with no-stick vegetable oil spray, dust lightly with garlic powder, and sprinkle fairly generously with lemon pepper. Place in the bag and bake as directed above.

Breast on the Bone

Use any of the above methods, but increase baking time to 25 minutes.

*Nutritional analysis isn't possible.

Quick Baked Chicken Breasts Italian Style

Spaghetti tossed with a drizzle of good olive oil and a clove of minced fresh garlic is an excellent accompaniment to this easily prepared chicken. A leafy green salad with sliced cucumber, mild white onion, and celery and shaved raw carrot curls tossed with a tangy Italian dressing would make this a complete meal. A nice bottle of Chianti wine wouldn't be amiss either!

Serves 2.

2	half chicken breasts, bone in but skinned
1	cup tomato juice
1	clove garlic, minced (or ½ teaspoon garlic powder)
½	teaspoon oregano
¼	teaspoon black pepper

Place the chicken breasts in a small shallow baking dish. Pour the tomato juice over the top. Sprinkle with the garlic, oregano, and pepper. Cover and bake in a preheated 350° oven for 45 minutes, or until done.

Each serving provides:

155	Calories	6 g	Carbohydrate
28 g	Protein	517 mg	Sodium
2 g	Fat	68 mg	Cholesterol

Fresh Rhubarb Breast of Chicken

The prolific rhubarb plant is chock full of potassium (212 mg in 1 cup cooked), and also contains vitamin C and fiber. Naturally we tried to team it up with chicken and came up with the following delicious combination — no kidding, it really is great!

Serves 3 to 4.

1	cup carrots, finely diced
½	cup green onions, sliced
2	whole chicken breasts, skinned, boned, and halved
	No-salt seasoning
¼	cup maple syrup
1	cup chicken stock
¼	teaspoon cinnamon
1	cup rhubarb, chopped
2	teaspoons cornstarch

Preheat oven to 350°. Sprinkle the carrots and green onions over the bottom of a small roasting pan. Place the chicken breasts on top of the vegetables and sprinkle with the no-salt seasoning. Drizzle 2 tablespoons of the maple syrup over the top. Cover and bake for 30 minutes. Remove the chicken breasts to a warm plate and keep warm while you complete the sauce.

To the roasting pan, add the chicken stock, the remaining 2 tablespoons maple syrup, the cinnamon, and rhubarb. Bring to a boil and cook gently until the rhubarb is tender. Stir in the cornstarch and continue to boil gently until thickened. Spoon the sauce over the chicken breasts and serve.

Each serving provides:

214	Calories	19 g	Carbohydrate
29 g	Protein	104 mg	Sodium
2 g	Fat	68 mg	Cholesterol

Rosemary Chicken Breasts

Quick and easy, with the lovely flavor of rosemary. Most people associate this herb with lamb, but it goes quite nicely with chicken as well.

Serves 6.

3	whole chicken breasts, bone in but skinned and halved
¾	cup low-fat yogurt
2	tablespoons lemon juice
1¼	teaspoons rosemary*
⅛	teaspoon black pepper
¼	cup finely crushed oat bran and wheat cereal**
	A few dashes of paprika
	Parsley for garnishing

Remove all visible fat from the chicken. Wash under cold running water and dry with paper towels. Arrange the breasts in a shallow baking dish. Combine the yogurt, lemon juice, rosemary, and pepper, stirring well. Spoon *half* of this mixture over the chicken. Bake, uncovered, in a preheated 375° oven for 45 minutes. Spoon the remaining yogurt mixture over the top and sprinkle with the cereal crumbs and paprika. Bake for an additional 10 minutes. Garnish with fresh parsley.

*If you have access to fresh rosemary, triple the amount.

**Cornflake crumbs may be substituted.

Each serving provides:

168	Calories	7 g	Carbohydrate
29 g	Protein	156 mg	Sodium
2 g	Fat	70 mg	Cholesterol

Stuffed Chicken Breast Winterburn

This is the perfect dinner entree for one or two . . . or more! It's easy to prepare and expands well. The quantities below are per serving.

Serves 1.

3   teaspoons soft margarine
1   generous tablespoon onion, chopped
½-⅔ cup bread crumbs
⅛   teaspoon celery seed
      Freshly ground black pepper to taste
1   teaspoon parsley, finely minced (or ¼ teaspoon dried
         parsley flakes)
½   teaspoon summer savory
1-2   teaspoons hot water (or stock)
1   half chicken breast, bone in but skinned
1   piece aluminum foil, about 12 inches square
1   scant teaspoon flour
      Paprika
      Parsley, finely minced (or dried parsley flakes)

Place 2 teaspoons of the margarine in the bottom of a small saucepan. Sauté the onion in the margarine until soft. Remove from heat and toss with the bread crumbs, celery seed, pepper, parsley, and summer savory. Add 1 or 2 teaspoons hot water (or stock) to the mixture, depending on how dry the bread crumbs are. You want the stuffing to be moist enough to hold together slightly. Form the dressing into a mound and press into the under-side of the chicken breast, well into the cavity formed by the rib cage. Place the stuffed chicken breast onto the foil. Rub the top of the breast with the remaining 1 teaspoon margarine. Sprinkle the flour over the top, patting it into the margarine a bit so it's ab-sorbed. Sprinkle with the paprika, black pepper, and minced parsley. Bring the ends of the foil together over the chicken. Seal the ends and top by folding the foil over into a tight package. Bake on a baking tray in a preheated 350° oven for 1 hour.

Freshly steamed peas and carrots would complete the meal.

Each serving provides:			
495	Calories	50 g	Carbohydrate
36 g	Protein	665 mg	Sodium
16 g	Fat	71 mg	Cholesterol

Stuffed Chicken Breasts
with Black Currant Sauce

Very nice for entertaining. You can make the chicken rolls and the sauce ahead of time but don't combine them until just before you put them in the oven.

Serves 8.

8   half chicken breasts, skinned and boned
1   clove garlic
½   pound ricotta (part skim milk) cheese
2   tablespoons reduced-calorie mayonnaise
        Freshly ground black pepper
3   tablespoons green onions, chopped

Place the chicken breasts between two pieces of plastic wrap and pound with a mallet (or the bottom of a wine bottle) until it's twice its original size and of uniform thickness. Rub one side of each piece with the garlic. Whip the ricotta cheese with the mayonnaise to a good spreading consistency, and spread over the same side of the chicken that you rubbed with the garlic. Sprinkle with the black pepper and top each with a good teaspoon of the green onions. Roll up the breasts, tucking in the ends so the filling doesn't escape, and place them seam side down in a 9 × 13-inch baking dish.

Black Currant Sauce

2   tablespoons brandy
1   cup black currant jam
2   tablespoons dry mustard
½   teaspoon basil, crushed
½   teaspoon rosemary, crushed

In a small bowl, combine the brandy, black currant jam, dry mustard (2 tablespoons seems like a lot, but you need it to give the sauce "zip"), basil, and rosemary. Spoon half of the sauce over the breasts, cover, and bake in a preheated 350° oven for 25 minutes. Remove the cover, spoon the remaining sauce over the chicken and bake for an additional 20 minutes, basting several times.

Each serving provides:			
296	Calories	30 g	Carbohydrate
31 g	Protein	138 mg	Sodium
5 g	Fat	78 mg	Cholesterol

Chicken Breasts Stuffed with Red Pepper Pesto

These chicken breasts are wonderful for entertaining. They are moist, flavorful, and lovely to look at. Advance preparation is important if you want to be "frazzle-free." You can get the breasts oven ready in the morning and the sauce can be made ahead and reheated. Leftover Red Pepper Pesto stuffed into mushroom caps makes a splendid hors d'oeuvre.*

Serves 8 to 12.

4-6   whole chicken breasts, skinned, boned, and halved
       No-stick vegetable oil spray

Red Pepper Pesto

1   cup hot water
3   large sweet red peppers, coarsely chopped
2   large cloves garlic, chopped
1   teaspoon dried basil (triple the amount if using fresh basil)
½   teaspoon no-salt seasoning
¼   teaspoon black pepper
½   cup freshly made bread crumbs (about 1½ slices bread, finely crumbled)
¼   cup Parmesan cheese, grated
2   tablespoons ground pine nuts (grind in a blender)

Pour the water into a 10-inch skillet. Add the peppers and garlic. Bring to a boil. Reduce heat and simmer for about 10 minutes, or until tender. Drain. Put the cooked peppers and garlic into a blender or food processor and puree. Return to the skillet. Add the basil, no-salt seasoning, and pepper and bring to a slow boil. Cook until all excess liquid is absorbed. Remove from heat and stir in the bread crumbs, cheese, and pine nuts.

Cut away any membranes or fat on the chicken. Place the chicken, one piece at a time, between two pieces of plastic wrap and flatten with a mallet to twice its original size. Place roughly 1 tablespoon of the Red Pepper Pesto in the center of each chicken piece and fold the edges of the chicken up over the filling to form a

---

*Any leftover pesto can be used to stuff mushroom caps for a terrific hors d'oeuvre. Place pesto-stuffed mushroom caps in a baking dish that has been sprayed with a no-stick vegetable oil spray. Bake in a preheated 350° oven for 8 to 10 minutes. Serve hot.

mound. Place in a shallow baking dish that's been sprayed with a no-stick vegetable oil spray. When ready to bake, spoon a little of the following Basil Cream Sauce on top of each breast and bake in a preheated 375° oven for 30 minutes. Serve the remaining sauce on the side.

Basil Cream Sauce

2	tablespoons flour
1	can (14 oz.) low-fat evaporated milk
1½	teaspoons dried basil (triple the amount if using fresh basil)
½	teaspoon lemon pepper
¼	teaspoon paprika
1	tablespoon sherry

Shake the flour in a jar with half of the evaporated milk until smooth. Pour into a small saucepan and stir in all of the remaining ingredients except the sherry. Cook over medium heat, stirring constantly, until thickened. Remove from heat and stir in the sherry.

Each serving provides:			
211	Calories	9 g	Carbohydrate
32 g	Protein	212 mg	Sodium
4 g	Fat	77 mg	Cholesterol

Potato Scallop Chicken Casserole

This dish is "soul food" — perfect for nights when you feel like a simple yet tasty meal. It's fairly colorless except for the slices of cooked tomato, so something bright like cooked, diced beets would be an excellent accompaniment. Add a crisp green salad to complete the meal.

Serves 4.

3   medium potatoes, peeled and sliced ¼ inch thick
2   medium onions, thinly sliced
3   tomatoes, sliced
        Salt or no-salt seasoning
        Freshly ground black pepper
4   half chicken breasts, boned and skinned
½   cup chicken stock
1   teaspoon dried rosemary (or 1 tablespoon fresh if available)
1   tablespoon soft margarine
        Paprika

Put a layer of potatoes into an 8-inch square casserole dish. Cover with a layer of the onions, then a layer of tomatoes. Season each layer well with salt or no-salt seasoning and pepper. Place the chicken breasts on top of the tomato layer. Top the chicken with another layer of potatoes, then onions, then tomatoes. Season these layers as well. End with a layer of potatoes. Add the chicken stock, sprinkle with the rosemary, and place small dabs of the soft margarine on top. Sprinkle with the paprika. Cover and bake for 1 hour in a preheated 350° oven, or until potatoes are tender. The cover may be removed during the last 10 minutes of baking to brown the top slightly.

Each serving provides:			
292	Calories	30 g	Carbohydrate
31 g	Protein	138 mg	Sodium
5 g	Fat	68 mg	Cholesterol

Cabbage Rolls Our Way

Cabbage rolls aren't something you're apt to find in a low-cholesterol chicken cookbook. We've taken the fat-laden beef out and put lean chicken breast in — with surprisingly good results.

Serves 8.

1	medium head of cabbage
3	half chicken breasts, boned and skinned
1½	cups quick-cooking rice, uncooked
1	small onion, minced
3	tablespoons fresh parsley, minced (or 1 tablespoon dried parsley flakes)
1	teaspoon dill
	No-stick vegetable oil spray
1	can (14 oz.) tomato sauce or crushed tomatoes
½	teaspoon pepper
1	tablespoon white wine vinegar
1	tablespoon brown sugar

Steam the cabbage until the leaves are transparent, or steam in the microwave.* Mince the chicken in a food processor or put through a meat grinder. Combine with the rice, onion, parsley, and dill. Put 1 teaspoon of the rice mixture in each cabbage leaf and roll up. Place the rolls in even layers in a casserole dish that has been sprayed with no-stick vegetable oil spray. Mix the tomato sauce, pepper, vinegar, and brown sugar together and pour over the cabbage rolls. Cover tightly and bake for 1½ hours in a preheated 350° oven.

*To prepare the cabbage in a microwave, place 1 cup water in the bottom of a round baking dish. Place the whole cabbage in the dish, cover with plastic wrap, and cook on high heat until the cabbage leaves are transparent. Time will vary according to the size of the cabbage. A medium cabbage will take approximately 30 to 40 minutes. Check at 10-minute intervals.

Each serving provides:			
151	Calories	23 g	Carbohydrate
13 g	Protein	124 mg	Sodium
1 g	Fat	26 mg	Cholesterol

Chicken Florentine Gates

A mixture of white and wild rice is nice served with this dish.

Serves 6.

1	tablespoon soft margarine
3	whole chicken breasts, skinned and boned
2	packages (10 oz. each) frozen spinach, thawed and drained
2	tablespoons lemon juice
½	teaspoon nutmeg
¼	cup Parmesan cheese (optional)*
1	tablespoon parsley, chopped
	Pepper to taste

Melt the margarine in a 9 × 13-inch baking dish (to melt put in the oven for 1 minute or in the microwave) to coat the bottom of the dish. Cut the chicken breasts in half and each half into 2 or 3 pieces. Place the chicken in the baking dish. Bake in a preheated 350° oven for 15 minutes. Remove the chicken from the dish and spread the spinach in the dish. Sprinkle with the lemon juice and nutmeg. Top the spinach with the chicken and cover with the following sauce. Sprinkle Parmesan cheese, parsley, and pepper on top and bake at 350° for 30 minutes.

*The Parmesan cheese can be cut to 1 or 2 tablespoons.

Sauce

2	tablespoons soft margarine
2	tablespoons flour
1	can (14 oz.) low-fat evaporated milk
1	teaspoon chicken bouillon mix
½	cup low-fat mozzarella cheese, grated
½	teaspoon nutmeg
1	teaspoon lemon pepper

Melt the margarine in a small saucepan. Add the flour and stir until bubbly. Gradually add the milk, stirring constantly until thickened. Stir in the chicken bouillon mix, cheese, nutmeg, and lemon pepper. Pour over the chicken.

Each serving provides:

301	Calories	14 g	Carbohydrate
38 g	Protein	676 mg	Sodium
10 g	Fat	84 mg	Cholesterol

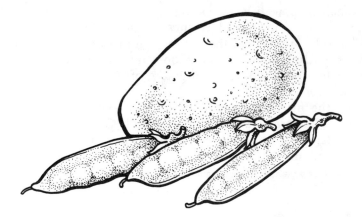

Cheese Stuffed Chicken Kiev

This Russian classic is traditionally deep-fried and bursts with garlic-laden butter when you cut into it. Those were the good old days, right? This low-calorie, low-fat version is certainly just as eye appealing and has a nice garlicky flavor. Enjoy!

Serves 8.

8	half chicken breasts, skinned and boned
½	teaspoon black pepper
3	cloves garlic, minced
4	green onions, finely minced
8	strips low-fat mozzarella cheese (about 2½ inches long, ½ inch wide, and ½ inch thick)
2	egg whites
2	teaspoons water
¼	cup flour
½	cup fine dry bread crumbs
1	tablespoon soft margarine
1	tablespoon olive oil

Pound the chicken breasts to about twice their original size. (The bottom of a cast-iron frying pan is great for this — just give a few whacks.) Sprinkle the chicken breasts with the pepper, a bit of the garlic, and a few minced green onions. Lay 1 strip of cheese in the center of each breast; fold the ends over, then roll up. Fasten with toothpicks. Repeat this procedure for the remaining breasts. In a small shallow dish, whisk the egg whites and water together. Place the flour and bread crumbs on separate plates. Dip the chicken rolls in the flour, then in the egg mixture, and then in the crumbs, coating evenly. Arrange on a rack (or a cake cooler) and refrigerate, uncovered, for a minimum of 20 minutes to allow the rolls to set.

Heat the margarine and olive oil in a skillet and brown the chicken rolls on all sides, turning carefully. Transfer to a shallow baking dish and bake, uncovered, in a preheated 350° oven for about 15 minutes.

Each serving provides:			
535	Calories	14 g	Carbohydrate
68 g	Protein	1,478 mg	Sodium
21 g	Fat*	124 mg	Cholesterol

*We know this looks high in fat, but it's actually a lower-fat version than the original — save it for special occasions.

Mandarin Chicken

Serves 4.

4	half chicken breasts, boned and skinned
	No-stick vegetable oil spray
⅓	cup corn syrup (dark or light)
1½	teaspoons lemon peel, grated
1½	teaspoons orange peel, grated
¼	cup lemon juice
2	teaspoons Dijon mustard*
¼	teaspoon curry powder
¼	teaspoon ground ginger
1	small can (10 oz.) mandarin oranges, drained

Place the chicken breasts in an 8-inch square baking dish that has been sprayed with no-stick vegetable oil spray. Combine all of the remaining ingredients, except the mandarin oranges, and spoon over the chicken breasts. Bake, uncovered, in a preheated 350° oven for 40 minutes, basting frequently. Add the orange segments during the last five minutes of baking over and around the chicken.

Note: This recipe doubles very well.

*Dijon mustard is high in sodium. If this is a problem for you, substitute low-sodium prepared mustard.

Each serving provides:

262	Calories	33 g	Carbohydrate
28 g	Protein	199 mg	Sodium
2 g	Fat	68 mg	Cholesterol

Fresh Mushroom Chicken Italian Style

Serve with hot rice, spaghetti, or linguini. Add a tossed green salad and a crusty loaf of Italian bread, and you have a fine meal.

Serves 4.

2	tablespoons flour
1	teaspoon no-salt seasoning
2	whole chicken breasts, skinned, boned, and halved
2	tablespoons olive oil
1	medium onion, chopped
2	large cloves garlic, minced
1	cup chicken stock
1¾	tablespoons tomato paste
1	teaspoon Italian seasoning*
2	cups fresh mushrooms, thickly sliced

Combine the flour and no-salt seasoning and coat the chicken breasts on both sides. Heat the oil in a 10-inch skillet and brown the chicken breasts lightly — 3 to 4 minutes on each side. Place in an 8-inch square shallow baking dish. Add the chopped onions to the skillet and sauté for about 2 minutes, or until they begin to color slightly, then add the garlic and sauté for an additional 1 minute. Stir in the remaining seasoned flour (there should be about 1 tablespoon left after coating the chicken). Stir in the chicken stock and bring to a slow boil. Stir in the tomato paste and, when well blended, stir in the Italian seasoning and the mushrooms. When the mushrooms are well coated, remove from heat and pour the mushrooms and sauce over the chicken breasts. Cover the dish with heavy foil or a lid and bake in a preheated 350° oven for 30 minutes, or until the chicken is done.

*Italian seasoning is a premixed blend of herbs containing marjoram, thyme, rosemary, savory, sage, oregano, and sweet basil.

Each serving provides:			
239	Calories	9 g	Carbohydrate
30 g	Protein	153 mg	Sodium
9 g	Fat	68 mg	Cholesterol

Baked Chicken Parmesan

Serves 4.

½   teaspoon freshly ground black pepper
½   teaspoon garlic powder
½   teaspoon paprika
½   teaspoon thyme
2   tablespoons Parmesan cheese
1   tablespoon dried parsley flakes
¼   cup fine bread crumbs
4   half chicken breasts, bone in but skinned
      No-stick vegetable oil spray
3   tablespoons water
3   tablespoons red wine

Place the seasonings, cheese, parsley, and bread crumbs in a small paper bag. Coat the chicken by shaking one or two pieces at a time in the bag. Spray a shallow baking dish with the no-stick vegetable oil spray. Add the water and arrange the chicken pieces in the dish. Spray the chicken with the no-stick vegetable oil spray and bake, uncovered, in a preheated 350° oven for 30 minutes. Drizzle the wine over the chicken, lower the oven temperature to 325°; cover with foil and bake for an additional 15 minutes. Remove foil, raise the oven temperature to 350°, and bake for another 10 minutes.

Each serving provides:

172	Calories	6 g	Carbohydrate
29 g	Protein	171 mg	Sodium
3 g	Fat	71 mg	Cholesterol

Chicken with Crushed Pineapple

Serves 4 to 6.

2   pounds chicken breasts, boned and skinned
½   cup crushed pineapple, drained
¼   cup pineapple juice (saved from the drained, crushed
        pineapple)
½   cup low-sodium soy sauce
¼   cup honey
¼   cup apple cider vinegar
5   teaspoons cornstarch
1   teaspoon fresh ginger, peeled and finely diced
1   clove garlic, minced
½   teaspoon black pepper

Remove all visible fat from the chicken. Wash under cold running water and dry. Cut into 1-inch cubes. Place in a baking pan. Spread the pineapple over the chicken. In a small saucepan, combine all of the remaining ingredients and bring to a boil, stirring constantly. Remove from heat and pour over the chicken. Bake in a preheated 375° oven for 20 minutes. Stir, then bake for an additional 20 minutes.

Serve with hot, fluffy rice.

Each serving provides:			
233	Calories	26 g	Carbohydrate
29 g	Protein	1,038 mg	Sodium
2 g	Fat	68 mg	Cholesterol

Raspberry Chicken

The wonderfully fresh and special flavor of raspberries comes through in this dish, making it lovely for entertaining.

Serves 6 to 8.

6-8 half chicken breasts, bone in but skinned
No-stick vegetable oil spray
Lemon pepper
1 tablespoon cornstarch
1 package (15 oz.) frozen raspberries, thawed and drained (reserve juice)
½ teaspoon cinnamon
1 teaspoon lemon juice

Spray the chicken breasts lightly with the oil. Sprinkle both sides with the lemon pepper. Place the breasts on a broiler rack and broil for 3 minutes per side.

Combine the cornstarch and the juice from the raspberries until smooth. Add the cinnamon and lemon juice. Heat this sauce in a small saucepan until thickened, stirring constantly, or microwave, whisking frequently until smooth. Add the raspberries.

Transfer the breasts to a casserole and spoon half of the sauce on top. Bake, covered, for 20 to 25 minutes. Uncover, add the remainder of the sauce, and bake for an additional 10 minutes.

Each serving provides:			
200	Calories	17 g	Carbohydrate
28 g	Protein	78 mg	Sodium
2 g	Fat	68 mg	Cholesterol

French Prune Rollups

Incredibly good, this dish is an invention of our friend David Brown, one of the best amateur cooks we know. The recipe is for two but can be easily expanded for an elegant dinner party. The rolls can be assembled in the morning and refrigerated until baking time.

Serves 2.

Filling

1	chicken thigh, skinned, boned, and minced
2	tablespoons low-fat yogurt
3	tablespoons prunes, chopped
1	teaspoon lemon juice
1	packet (2 teaspoons) sugar substitute
2	tablespoons wheat germ
½	teaspoon oregano
½	teaspoon black pepper
¼	teaspoon cinnamon

Mix all of the filling ingredients well and chill for at least 1 hour in the refrigerator.

2	half chicken breasts, boned and skinned
	No-stick vegetable oil spray
4	tablespoons white wine
	A few chopped prunes
	Lemon pepper

Flatten the chicken breasts between two pieces of plastic wrap with a mallet (or the bottom of a wine bottle). Shape the filling into two "sausages" and roll one up in each breast. Place seam side down in a baking dish that has been sprayed with a no-stick veg-etable oil spray. Pour the white wine on top and garnish with more chopped prunes (roughly 2 teaspoons per breast) and sprinkle with the lemon pepper. Bake, covered, in a preheated 350° oven for 45 minutes. Uncover and bake for an additional 5 minutes. To serve, slice each roll diagonally into ½- to 1-inch pieces.

Good accompaniments would be wild rice and green beans or fettucine with a bit of olive oil, garlic, and Parmesan cheese. A tossed green salad and a baguette of French bread would complete the meal.

Each serving provides:

248	Calories	15 g	Carbohydrate
37 g	Protein	120 mg	Sodium
4 g	Fat	98 mg	Cholesterol

Ollie's Spinach and Chicken Rolls in Tomato Sauce

A great dinner party dish.

Serves 8.

8	half chicken breasts, boned, skinned, and all visible fat removed
1	large clove garlic, minced
2	teaspoons canola or safflower oil
1	package (10 oz.) frozen spinach, thawed, drained, and chopped
1	can (10 oz.) mushroom pieces, drained
½	teaspoon no-salt seasoning
1	cup low-fat mozzarella cheese, grated*
1	teaspoon brown sugar
1	large can (28 oz.) tomatoes, crushed

Lay the chicken breasts between two sheets of plastic and pound with a mallet (or the bottom of a wine bottle) until flattened to about ½ inch thick. In a skillet, sauté the garlic in the oil, add the spinach and mushrooms, and combine while heating through. Sprinkle the breasts with a bit of no-salt seasoning and spoon 2 tablespoons of the spinach mixture onto each breast. Top with 1 tablespoon grated cheese. Roll up securely and fasten with tooth-picks. In the same skillet, lightly brown the chicken rolls on all sides. Transfer to a large, shallow baking dish. Add the brown sugar to the tomatoes and spoon on top and around the sides of the chicken. Bake, covered, in a preheated 350° oven for 40 minutes. Uncover and bake an additional 15 minutes.

*One quarter pound cheese yields 1 cup grated.

Each serving provides:			
206	Calories	8 g	Carbohydrate
33 g	Protein	467 mg	Sodium
4 g	Fat	73 mg	Cholesterol

Chicken and Onion Stacks

Serves 2.

1	whole chicken breast, boned and skinned
2	tablespoons oat bran
¼	teaspoon no-salt seasoning
¼	teaspoon garlic powder
	No-stick vegetable oil spray
4	slices tomato
	Celery seed
4	thin slices low-fat mozzarella cheese
4	tablespoons green onions, chopped
2	tablespoons white wine or chicken stock
	Lemon pepper

Cut the chicken breast in half, then in half again to get 4 pieces. Place each piece between two sheets of wax paper and pound with a mallet to about half its original thickness. Combine the oat bran, no-salt seasoning, and garlic powder. Dip the chicken in the oat bran mixture. Spray a non-stick frying pan with no-stick vegetable oil spray and sauté the chicken for about 2 minutes on each side. Place the chicken in a shallow baking dish in a single layer. Arrange 1 slice of tomato on top of each piece of chicken. Sprinkle the chicken lightly with the celery seed. Place 1 slice of cheese on each piece of chicken, then top each piece with 1 tablespoon of green onions. Add the wine or chicken stock to the bottom of the dish. Add lemon pepper to taste. Bake, covered, in a preheated 350° oven for 15 to 20 minutes.

Each serving provides:			
289	Calories	8 g	Carbohydrate
43 g	Protein	561 mg	Sodium
9 g	Fat	88 mg	Cholesterol

DARK MEAT

Cajun Drums

We found the seasoning just about right, but if you're the type who likes a 3-alarm fire going off in your mouth, by all means add more Cajun spice! If your local supermarket does not carry Cajun spice, it's a simple matter to make your own (see below). Make ahead of time and use as needed. It could make a thoughtful gift as well.

Serves 6.

12   chicken drumsticks, skinned
        No-stick vegetable oil spray
½   cup flour
1   teaspoon Cajun spice

Sauce

1   cup low-salt ketchup
1   tablespoon prepared horseradish
1   teaspoon onion powder
1   clove garlic, minced (or 1 teaspoon garlic powder)
1   teaspoon Cajun spice

Lightly spray the drumsticks with the oil. Combine the flour and Cajun spice. Roll the drumsticks in the flour, coating well. Refrigerate at least 30 minutes, or until needed (up to 24 hours). Broil the drumsticks 4 minutes per side, or until well browned.

Combine all of the sauce ingredients. Brush or spoon onto the drumsticks. Place in a shallow casserole dish in a single layer. Bake, uncovered, in a preheated 350° oven for 30 to 35 minutes. Continue to brush the sauce on the drumsticks while they are baking, turning every 10 minutes.

Cajun Spice

1	tablespoon paprika
¾	teaspoon cayenne pepper
½	teaspoon *each* white pepper, black pepper, dry mustard, and garlic powder
¼	teaspoon *each* oregano and thyme
	Pinch of crushed bay leaf

Mix all of the ingredients together and store in a dry place. You can use this to give a little zing to soup, sauces, etc., instead of salt.

Each serving provides:			
239	Calories	20 g	Carbohydrate
27 g	Protein	129 mg	Sodium
5 g	Fat	95 mg	Cholesterol

Plum Drumsticks

These spicy-sweet drumsticks disappeared like hot cakes when we served them at a recipe testing. Some rice and green beans or a salad would complete the meal.

Serves 4.

8	chicken drumsticks, skinned
½	cup plum jam
1	tablespoon low-sodium soy sauce
1	teaspoon dry mustard
¼	teaspoon cayenne pepper
2	tablespoons lemon juice
1	teaspoon horseradish
1	tablespoon dehydrated onion
¼	cup tomato paste

Place the drumsticks in a single layer in a shallow baking dish. Place all of the remaining ingredients in a small saucepan and heat until the jam has melted and the liquid comes to a simmer. Spoon on top of the chicken. Cover loosely and bake in a preheated 350° oven for 1 hour.

Each serving provides:

280	Calories	33 g	Carbohydrate
27 g	Protein	503 mg	Sodium
5 g	Fat	95 mg	Cholesterol

Hot Mango Drumsticks

Serves 8.

1	can (14 oz.) sliced mangoes, drained but save 1 tablespoon juice*
½	cup peach jam
1	tablespoon lemon juice
¼	teaspoon powdered ginger
2	teaspoons cornstarch
1	tablespoon mango juice (see above)
¾	teaspoon crushed red pepper flakes
4	pounds chicken drumsticks (16 to 18 drumsticks), skin and all visible fat removed

Chop the mangoes well. Transfer to a small saucepan and stir in the jam, lemon juice, and ginger. Stir the cornstarch into the 1 tablespoon mango juice and add to the saucepan. Bring to a boil, then turn heat down to medium and stir until the mixture thickens. Remove from heat and stir in the crushed red pepper flakes.

Place the chicken drumsticks in a shallow baking pan and spoon the sauce over the top. Cover and bake in a preheated 350° oven for 40 minutes. Remove the cover and bake an additional 35 minutes, basting with sauce several times.

*You can substitute 1 large fresh mango (peeled, seeded, and chopped) and 1 tablespoon orange juice for the canned mango.

Each serving provides:

226	Calories	21 g	Carbohydrate
26 g	Protein	113 mg	Sodium
4 g	Fat	94 mg	Cholesterol

Pygmy Drumsticks

Drumettes are the top meaty half of chicken wings. Not all supermarkets carry them, but many do. Good "finger food," they're perfect for a cocktail party or a Spanish-style tapas party.

Makes 8 to 10 appetizer-size servings.

⅓	cup low-sodium soy sauce
2	tablespoons honey
2	tablespoons apple cider vinegar
1	tablespoon minced fresh ginger (or 1 teaspoon powdered ginger)
1	tablespoon sesame oil
2	cloves garlic, minced
3	pounds (approximately 2 dozen) chicken drumettes, skinned
	No-stick vegetable oil spray (optional)
	Sesame seeds

Combine all of the ingredients except the chicken and sesame seeds. Mix well and pour over the chicken pieces. Marinate for at least two hours at room temperature, or overnight in the refrigerator.

Place the drumettes on racks on two baking pans that have been sprayed with a no-stick vegetable oil spray or lined with foil (this makes cleanup easier). Sprinkle with the sesame seeds. Bake in a preheated 425° oven for 30 minutes. Serve warm or at room temperature.

These chicken drumettes can be baked up to one day ahead and stored, covered, in the refrigerator. If desired, reheat in a preheated 350° oven for about 10 minutes.

Each serving provides:

157	Calories	3 g	Carbohydrate
23 g	Protein	319 mg	Sodium
5 g	Fat	60 mg	Cholesterol

Sweet and Sour Drumsticks

Serves 4.

	No-stick vegetable oil spray
3	pounds chicken drumsticks, skinned
¾	cup chicken stock
2	tablespoons low-sodium soy sauce
½	cup honey
1	clove garlic, minced (or ½ to 1 teaspoon garlic powder)
1	teaspoon fresh ginger, grated (or ½ teaspoon ground ginger)
2	tablespoons white wine vinegar
	Paprika
	Parsley, finely chopped

Spray a 9 × 13-inch baking pan with no-stick vegetable oil spray and arrange the drumsticks in a single layer. Combine all of the remaining ingredients, except the paprika and parsley, in a small bowl (or shake in a glass jar). Pour the sauce over the chicken. Sprinkle with the paprika and minced parsley. Bake, uncovered, in a preheated 325° oven for 1 to 1½ hours, or until done. Turn halfway though baking and sprinkle with additional paprika and parsley.

Each serving provides:

325	Calories	37 g	Carbohydrate
33 g	Protein	447 mg	Sodium
6 g	Fat	118 mg	Cholesterol

Sweet Chinese Style Drumsticks

Serves 8 to 10.

This dish is perfect for a large buffet. You get it oven ready in the morning or the night before. The drumsticks have a nice sweet taste as well as an appetizing glaze. Reduce the proportions and it makes a tasty family meal as well.

3	tablespoons sugar
1½	teaspoons Chinese five spice powder*
3	tablespoons hoisin sauce
3	tablespoons sesame oil
3	tablespoons Chinese cooking wine (or sherry)
5	pounds (roughly 18 pieces) drumsticks, skinned
6	tablespoons corn syrup (light or dark)

Mix all of the ingredients (except the drumsticks and corn syrup) into a paste and rub well on the drumsticks. Marinate for 2 to 3 hours, or overnight in the refrigerator. Bake in a preheated 350° oven for 45 minutes, or until done. Remove from the oven and brush with the corn syrup. Place under a preheated broiler for 2 to 3 minutes for a nice glazed appearance.

*Chinese five spice powder can be found in most supermarkets, but if you want to make your own, stir together 1 teaspoon ground cinnamon, 1 teaspoon crushed anise seed (or 1 whole star anise, crushed), ¼ teaspoon crushed fennel seed, ¼ teaspoon freshly ground black pepper, and ⅛ teaspoon ground cloves. Store the mixture in an airtight container in a cool dry place. Makes about 1 tablespoon.

Each serving provides:			
268	Calories	16 g	Carbohydrate
28 g	Protein	341 mg	Sodium
9 g	Fat	105 mg	Cholesterol

Crunchy Oat Bran Drumsticks

Even if you don't normally buy buttermilk, a special purchase is worth it for this dish. You can always make muffins with the leftover milk, but we bet you'll be rushing out to get more drumsticks to make these tasty morsels again.

Serves 4 to 5 (about 2 drumsticks per person).

8-10	chicken drumsticks (from fryers), skinned
1½	cups buttermilk
½	cup whole wheat bread crumbs
2	tablespoons sesame seeds
½	cup oat bran
1	teaspoon no-salt seasoning or salt
1	teaspoon garlic powder
¼	cup grated Parmesan cheese
	No-stick vegetable oil spray

Soak the drumsticks in the buttermilk for about 1 hour. Mix the bread crumbs, sesame seeds, oat bran, no-salt seasoning, garlic powder, and Parmesan cheese in a bowl or plastic bag. Coat the chicken with this mixture, piece by piece, and place on a cookie sheet that you've sprayed lightly with the no-stick vegetable oil spray. Just before placing in the oven, spray the chicken lightly with oil as well. Bake in the upper third of a preheated 350° oven, uncovered, for 1 hour.

Each serving provides:			
265	Calories	15 g	Carbohydrate
33 g	Protein	842 mg	Sodium
10 g	Fat	101 mg	Cholesterol

Fruit and Fiber Stuffed Chicken Legs

It can be difficult to get great flavor in a chicken dish when the skin, butter, and salt are eliminated, but we think you'll find these chicken legs don't suffer in the least. Your guests won't even realize that you've done them the kindness of removing so many excess calories from their entrée.

Serves 4.

4	large (2 to 2½ pounds) chicken legs (thighs and drumsticks intact), skinned
2	tablespoons margarine
3	tablespoons green onions, finely sliced (include a bit of the green tops)
¼	cup celery, chopped (include a few leaves)
½-¾	cup freshly made whole wheat bread crumbs
¼	teaspoon no-salt seasoning
¼	teaspoon freshly ground pepper
6	prunes, pitted and coarsely chopped
¼	cup white wine (or apple juice)

Preheat the oven to 325°. With the point of a sharp knife, make a pocket along the fleshy side of each thigh extending the pocket under the thigh bone and almost through to the other side (it's best to turn the leg fleshiest side down for this). In a small skillet, melt the margarine and sauté the onions and celery over low heat until soft but not browned.

In a small bowl, combine the bread crumbs, no-salt seasoning, pepper, sautéed onion and celery, and coarsely chopped prunes.

Stuff each leg's pocket with about one quarter of the stuffing. Fasten closed with toothpicks. Place the legs in a casserole dish so the legs barely touch one another. Pour the wine in the bottom of the dish. Cover tightly and bake for 1½ hours.

Each serving provides:			
259	Calories	12 g	Carbohydrate
27 g	Protein	236 mg	Sodium
11 g	Fat	104 mg	Cholesterol

Chicken with 30 Cloves of Garlic

Yes . . . that's 30 cloves! Garlic's legendary reputation as a natural high blood pressure medicine, among other healthful properties, led to the creation of the following dish. Roasting garlic eliminates its characteristic bite and it tastes very mellow. A dry red wine is perfect with this dish.

Serves 6 to 8.

30	cloves garlic, peeled
8-10	pieces of chicken, drumsticks and thighs, skin and all visible fat removed*
1	tablespoon olive oil
1	tablespoon parsley, minced
1	teaspoon oregano
1	teaspoon basil
3	tablespoons dry vermouth (or white wine)

The garlic cloves can be popped into the microwave for about 10 seconds to make peeling a little easier, or pour hot water over the cloves for just a few seconds to loosen the skins, so they can be pulled off easily with a paring knife.

Place half of the garlic cloves in the bottom of a baking dish. Place the chicken pieces on top. Drizzle with the olive oil and sprinkle with the parsley, oregano, and basil. Add the vermouth and sprinkle the remaining cloves of garlic on top. Seal the dish very tightly with heavy-duty aluminum foil. If the dish has a lid, place the lid on top of the foil. Bake in a preheated 250° oven for 3 hours. You can then either transfer the chicken to a heated platter, mash the garlic into any pan juices, and spoon over the chicken, or you can simply bring the dish from the oven to the table and serve the whole cloves of garlic with the chicken. You'll love them! Really!

*Thighs are sneaky; they hide little pockets of fat, so search carefully and remove as much as possible.

Each serving provides:			
163	Calories	5 g	Carbohydrate
23 g	Protein	97 mg	Sodium
5 g	Fat	83 mg	Cholesterol

Chicken à l'Orange

If you have a cholesterol problem, duck (alas) is a no-no. However, you can use the hind quarters of chicken and come up with a delicious Chicken à l'Orange.

Serves 4.

2	medium oranges, thinly sliced
4	chicken quarters, dark meat only, skinned
	Sprinkling of no-salt seasoning and pepper
1½	cups orange marmalade
½	cup plus 2 tablespoons honey
1¼	teaspoons cinnamon
¾	teaspoon ground cloves
2½	teaspoons rosemary
⅓	cup orange juice

Place the sliced oranges in the bottom of a shallow baking pan. Arrange the chicken on top of the orange slices. Sprinkle with no-salt seasoning and pepper. Combine the orange marmalade, honey, cinnamon, cloves, and rosemary. Brush about one third of this sauce over the chicken. Place the baking pan into a larger shallow pan of hot water (so the sauce won't burn on the bottom). There should be about 1 inch of water in the outer pan. Bake in a preheated 350° oven for 1½ hours, basting every 30 minutes. In a saucepan, add the orange juice to the remaining sauce and bring to a boil. Serve the sauce on the side.

Note: This recipe doubles well.

Each serving provides:

675	Calories	140 g	Carbohydrate
28 g	Protein	133 mg	Sodium
5 g	Fat	104 mg	Cholesterol

Chicken Thighs with Red Wine and Pimientos

Serves 6.

2-3   tablespoons safflower oil
6-7   small (about 2 pounds) chicken thighs, skin and fat removed*
        Freshly ground black pepper
1   large onion, finely chopped
1   small can (4 oz.) pimientos, drained and chopped
½   cup dry red wine

Heat 2 tablespoons of the oil in a 10-inch skillet and brown the thighs quickly. Sprinkle with freshly ground black pepper and place in a baking dish in a single layer. Add the chopped onion to the skillet and sauté until the onion is soft but not brown (there should still be enough oil in the skillet for this; if not, add no more than 1 additional tablespoon). Add the pimientos and cook for a minute or two, mixing well with the onion. Add the wine and let it boil for 1 minute on high heat, stirring constantly. Spoon the sauce over the chicken thighs. Cover tightly and bake in a pre-heated 350° oven for 1¼ hours.

*Chicken thighs have hidden pockets of fat so search them carefully.

Each serving provides:			
158	Calories	3 g	Carbohydrate
17 g	Protein	80 mg	Sodium
8 g	Fat	72 mg	Cholesterol

LIGHT AND DARK MEAT
(WHOLE CHICKEN)

Whole Chicken, Half Baked, Half Steamed

Serves 4.

3   pound whole roasting chicken
     No-salt seasoning

Rinse and wipe the chicken. Remove and discard any fat that can be pulled away from the body cavity or from under the skin. Sprinkle the cavity of the chicken with no-salt seasoning. Fold the wing tips back under the bird, then tie the wings and legs close to the body. Place the chicken on a broiler rack or a broiler pan. Pour about ¼ inch of water into the bottom of the pan. Cover loosely with foil and bake in a preheated 350° oven for 2 hours.

Remove the skin and serve hot. Any leftovers can be served cold with the following sauce for dipping.

Low-Calorie Dipping Sauce

¾   cup low-fat yogurt
1   tablespoon lemon juice
½   package sugar substitute
¼   teaspoon dry mustard
1½   teaspoons dill
½   clove garlic, minced

Combine all of the above ingredients thoroughly. This is best made ahead of time to allow flavors to blend.

Each 1 tablespoon of dipping sauce provides:

10	Calories	1 g	Carbohydrate
1 g	Protein	11 mg	Sodium
0 g	Fat	1 mg	Cholesterol

Glazed Broiler Halves

Serves 4.

1   jar (8 oz.) red currant jelly
1   cup orange juice
2   small (about 3 pounds total) broilers, cut in half and skinned
        Salt (or salt substitute) and pepper to taste

In a small saucepan, melt the currant jelly in the orange juice
and bring to a boil. Remove from heat. Place the broiler halves in
a shallow roasting pan and brush with the glaze. Bake in a preheated 350° oven for 1½ hours, basting frequently, until all of the
sauce is used. You can eliminate any risk of the sauce burning by
placing the baking pan in a larger pan filled with about 1 inch of
water. Otherwise bake the chicken in the upper third of the oven.
Add salt and pepper to taste.

Note: This is a nice glaze for Rock Cornish game hens as well.

Each serving provides:			
453	Calories	47 g	Carbohydrate
42 g	Protein	133 mg	Sodium
11 g	Fat	127 mg	Cholesterol

Stuffed Rock Cornish Game Hens

The wonderfully moist meat and fiber-rich dressing of these small birds will more than compensate you for having to forego the skin. Remember to line the baking dish with foil before baking for easy cleanup (honey has a tendency to burn). This recipe can be cut in half, making this a very easy dinner for two.

Serves 4.

2½   tablespoons black currants
3   slices whole wheat or multi-grained bread, toasted
1   mandarin orange, peeled, sectioned, and cut into bite-size
          pieces
¼   teaspoon sage
2   Rock Cornish game hens

Pour boiling water over the currants and let them soften while you prepare the rest of the stuffing. Break the toast up into coarse crumbs. Toss with the mandarin orange, sage, and drained currants. Rinse the hens well and pat them dry. Remove any excess fat. Fill the cavities with the stuffing and sew up the opening or skewer it closed securely. Tie the legs together and tie the wings to the body (you'll remove these strings before serving). Bake in a preheated 350° oven for 1½ hours, basting frequently with the following sauce.

Basting Sauce

¼   cup honey
½   cup orange juice
1   teaspoon grated orange rind (optional)
½   teaspoon ginger

Combine the sauce ingredients and heat until the honey is liquified and mixes well with the other ingredients. Brush over the hens at 15-minute intervals. To serve, remove the strings and cut the hens in half. Game shears are perfect for this. (If you plan on making chicken a big part of your diet, you would be wise to invest in this handy tool.) Skin the hens before serving.

Each serving provides:			
445	Calories	35 g	Carbohydrate
36 g	Protein	214 mg	Sodium
18 g	Fat*	110 mg	Cholesterol

*Although this is mostly the "good" type of fat, you may want to save this recipe for a special occasion.

Jamaican Chicken

On a recent trip to Jamaica we watched our very competent native cook prepare this dish. It was fascinating — the chicken takes on a rich mahogany color when it's sautéed with the melted brown sugar. It is absolutely delicious.

Serves 4.

1	cup onion, finely chopped
2	tablespoons green onions, sliced (including some of the green tops)
1	large clove garlic, minced
¼	teaspoon thyme
1	teaspoon no-salt seasoning
⅛	teaspoon freshly ground black pepper
1	tablespoon white wine vinegar
2	tablespoons Worcestershire sauce
2½-3	pounds chicken parts, skin and all visible fat removed
2	tablespoons olive oil
2	tablespoons firmly packed dark brown sugar
1	can (14 oz.) tomatoes, drained (discard juice then puree the tomatoes)
1½	tablespoons ketchup

In a large bowl, combine the onion, green onions, garlic, thyme, no-salt seasoning, pepper, vinegar, and Worcestershire sauce. Add the chicken, turning to coat it well. Place in the refrigerator to marinate for at least 1 hour — longer is better. When ready to cook, remove the chicken from the marinade and shake any excess marinade back into the bowl. In a large heavy-bottomed skillet, heat the olive oil over moderately high heat until hot (but not too hot). Add the brown sugar. When the sugar has melted, immediately add the chicken and sauté on both sides until it becomes a rich brown color. (The chicken will "spit" a bit when it first hits the hot pan, as will the marinade.) Transfer the chicken to a baking dish. Add the reserved marinade to the skillet and cook, stirring over moderate heat, until all of the browned bits from the bottom are scraped up and integrated into the sauce — about 2 minutes.

Stir in the pureed tomatoes and the ketchup. Spoon the sauce over the chicken and bake, covered, in a preheated 350° oven for 1 hour.
   Serve with rice or mashed potatoes.

Each serving provides:			
316	Calories	18 g	Carbohydrate
34 g	Protein	430 mg	Sodium
12 g	Fat	105 mg	Cholesterol

Fresh Orange Chicken

Serves 4.

¼   cup whole wheat flour
½   teaspoon paprika
2½-3 pounds chicken parts, skinned
2   tablespoons canola or safflower oil
    Freshly ground pepper
    No-salt seasoning
1   small clove garlic, minced (or ½ teaspoon garlic powder)
½   cup mild, red chili sauce
1   cup orange juice
¼   cup green pepper, chopped
1   tablespoon molasses
1   tablespoon prepared mustard
2   medium oranges, peeled and sliced into half cartwheels

Place two tablespoons of the whole wheat flour into a plastic or brown paper bag. Add the paprika. Shake the chicken pieces to coat lightly. In a large skillet, brown the chicken pieces in the oil. Transfer to a shallow baking dish. Sprinkle with the freshly ground pepper and no-salt seasoning to taste. Stir the remaining 2 tablespoons of flour and the garlic into the chili sauce. Add all of the remaining ingredients (except the oranges) to the sauce and pour over the chicken. Bake, covered, in a preheated 350° oven for 50 minutes. Remove the cover and arrange the orange slices on top of the chicken. Replace the cover and bake for an additional 10 minutes.

Each serving provides:			
381	Calories	34 g	Carbohydrate
35 g	Protein	623 mg	Sodium
12 g	Fat	105 mg	Cholesterol

Orange and Onion Chicken

Serves 8.

5-6   pounds chicken parts, skin and all visible fat removed
2   tablespoons flour
       Freshly ground black pepper
2   tablespoons safflower oil
       Zest of 1 orange, julienned
3   medium onions, thinly sliced
1   teaspoon thyme
1¾   cups orange juice
2   tablespoons fresh lemon juice
1   tablespoon honey
¾   cup dry white wine

Dust the chicken pieces with the flour. Grind some black pepper on top. In a large, heavy-bottomed skillet, heat the oil over medium-high heat and sauté the chicken in several batches until golden brown; 4 to 5 minutes on each side. Transfer the chicken to a 9 × 13-inch baking dish and scatter the orange zest on top. Deglaze the skillet with 2 tablespoons of water and cook the onions, stirring occasionally, until they are translucent; 5 to 8 minutes. Stir in the thyme and spread this mixture over the chicken.

Mix together the orange juice, lemon juice, honey, and wine in the skillet and bring to a boil over high heat. Let boil until the liquid is reduced to about 1 cup. Pour the sauce over the chicken. Bake, uncovered, in a preheated 350° oven, basting once with the sauce, until the juices run clear when a thigh is pierced with the tip of a sharp knife (about 45 to 55 minutes).

Each serving provides:			
262	Calories	13 g	Carbohydrate
33 g	Protein	118 mg	Sodium
8 g	Fat	105 mg	Cholesterol

Crumb Crisped Chicken

Serves 4.

2   pounds chicken parts
⅓   cup low-fat milk
⅔   cup Crumb Coating (see below)

Skin the chicken pieces and remove any visible fat. Dip the pieces in the milk, then roll in the crumb coating. Place in a single layer on a shallow, foil-lined (9 × 13-inch) baking pan. A light spray with a no-stick vegetable oil spray will give the crumbs an even crispier texture. Bake in a preheated 400° oven until the large pieces are fork-tender (about 40 minutes). Turn once for even browning.

Crumb Coating

2   cups fine whole wheat bread crumbs*
¼   cup flour
2½   teaspoons paprika
1   teaspoon salt or no-salt seasoning
2   teaspoons oregano leaves
1   teaspoon onion salt
1   teaspoon garlic powder
1   teaspoon sugar
½   teaspoon ground oregano

Mix the crumb coating ingredients together thoroughly. Store in a tightly covered container. Makes 2½ cups. Use about ⅓ cup per pound of poultry. This keeps three to four weeks in the refrigerator.

*We used Roman Meal brand thin-sliced bread. Eight slices of bread made 2 cups of crumbs.

Each serving provides:			
168	Calories	7 g	Carbohydrate
25 g	Protein	571 mg	Sodium
4 g	Fat	77 mg	Cholesterol

Chicken Oregano

This popular dish is of Greek origin. We use considerably less oil than the Greeks, but the marinating allows the flavors of lemon, oregano, and garlic to permeate the flesh, resulting in very tasty chicken. So who needs the extra oil? It's delicious cold as well. Take some along to your next picnic.

Serves 4.

2½-3 pounds chicken parts, skin and all visible fat removed
1   tablespoon oregano
¼   cup lemon juice
2   tablespoons olive oil
1   medium onion, sliced and separated into rings
1   clove garlic, minced
      Paprika
      Lemon for garnishing

Wash the chicken under cold running water and pat dry with paper towels. Combine the oregano, lemon juice, olive oil, onion, and garlic. Pour over the chicken, mixing well, and marinate in the refrigerator for a minimum of 3 hours. When ready to bake, place in a shallow baking dish (marinade and all), sprinkle well with the paprika, and bake in a preheated 350° oven, uncovered, for 1 hour.

Thin slices of fresh lemon make a nice garnish for this dish.

Each serving provides:			
252	Calories	3 g	Carbohydrate
32 g	Protein	119 mg	Sodium
12 g	Fat	105 mg	Cholesterol

Trudy's Oven Barbecued Chicken

Serves 8.

	No-stick vegetable oil spray
2	large onions, chopped
½	cup ketchup
1	cup water
1	tablespoon Worcestershire sauce
1	tablespoon sugar
1	tablespoon white wine vinegar
1	teaspoon no-salt seasoning
1	teaspoon dry mustard
½	teaspoon chili powder
	Dash of Tabasco sauce
2	whole fryers, cut into pieces and skinned

Spray a Teflon frying pan well with the no-stick vegetable oil spray and sauté the onions until soft. Mix with all of the remaining ingredients, except the chicken. Wash the chicken, remove any visible fat, and dry well. Place the chicken in a large baking dish and pour the sauce on top. Bake, covered, in a preheated 350° oven for 1½ hours. Remove the cover and bake for an additional ½ hour.

Each serving provides:

221	Calories	9 g	Carbohydrate
33 g	Protein	319 mg	Sodium
5 g	Fat	105 mg	Cholesterol

Sticky Chicken

Serves 4.

6   pieces (2½ pounds) chicken parts, skin and all visible fat
    removed
    Garlic powder
    Ginger
    No-salt seasoning
2   tablespoons brown sugar
2   tablespoons low-sodium soy sauce
2   tablespoons honey

Place the chicken in a shallow baking dish. Sprinkle to taste
with the garlic powder, ginger, and no-salt seasoning. Sprinkle 1
teaspoon brown sugar over each piece of chicken and spoon 1
teaspoon soy sauce over each piece. Bake in a preheated 375° oven
for 45 minutes. Remove from the oven and drizzle 1 teaspoon
honey over each piece. Return to the oven and bake for an additional 15 minutes, or until golden brown.

Each serving provides:

247	Calories	16 g	Carbohydrate
35 g	Protein	426 mg	Sodium
4 g	Fat	112 mg	Cholesterol

Millie's Raisin and Peach Chicken

Serves 12.

1	tablespoon soft margarine
¼	cup onion, chopped
2	tablespoons brown sugar
½	cup mild red chili sauce
1	jar (4½ oz.) strained peaches*
½	cup water
¼	cup golden raisins
1½	teaspoons Worcestershire sauce
12	pieces (5 pounds) chicken, skin and all visible fat removed
1	can (14 oz.) sliced peaches, drained

Melt the margarine in a saucepan. Add the onion and cook until tender but not browned. Stir in the brown sugar, chili sauce, strained peaches, water, raisins, and Worcestershire sauce. Bring to a boil and cook for 3 to 5 minutes. Place the chicken in a shallow baking pan. Spoon the sauce over the chicken. Garnish with the sliced peaches. Bake, uncovered, in a preheated 350° oven for approximately 1½ hours, or until done. Baste occasionally.

*Buy a small jar in the baby food section, or puree canned peaches well in the blender to get a generous ½ cup.

Each serving provides:			
188	Calories	15 g	Carbohydrate
24 g	Protein	257 mg	Sodium
4 g	Fat	75 mg	Cholesterol

Sweet and Sour Chicken

Always a hit.

Serves 4.

3	pound chicken, cut into pieces
	No-stick vegetable oil spray
	Lemon pepper
1	can (14 oz.) pineapple chunks, well drained (save the juice)
1	cup sugar
2	tablespoons cornstarch
½	teaspoon fresh ginger, grated (or ¼ teaspoon ground ginger)
¾	cup white wine vinegar
1	tablespoon low-sodium soy sauce
1	chicken bouillon cube
1	large green pepper, cut into ½-inch strips

Remove the skin and all visible fat from the chicken. Wash under cold running water and dry well. Spray a large skillet well with the no-stick vegetable oil spray. Brown the chicken on both sides. Sprinkle the lemon pepper on top of the chicken halfway through the browning process. Add water to the reserved pineapple juice to make 1¼ cups liquid. In a medium saucepan, combine the sugar, cornstarch, and ginger. Stir in the pineapple liquid, vinegar, soy sauce, and bouillon cube. Cook over medium heat, stirring, until the mixture thickens and comes to a boil. Boil for 3 minutes, then remove from heat. Place the browned chicken in one layer in a flat, shallow baking dish and pour the sauce over the top. Bake, uncovered, in a preheated 350° oven for 30 minutes. Baste with the sauce. Add the pineapple chunks and green pepper strips and bake for an additional 30 minutes, or until the chicken is tender.

Serve with hot, fluffy rice.

	Each serving provides:		
480	Calories	73 g	Carbohydrate
36 g	Protein	555 mg	Sodium
6 g	Fat	115 mg	Cholesterol

Apple, Cinnamon, and Raisin Chicken

An experiment reported in Reader's Digest *(April 1989) tells of 30 middle-aged men and women who ate two or three apples every day for a month, resulting in a drop in blood cholesterol for 80 percent of the group. In half of this group, the cholesterol level dropped by more than 10 percent. When you're buying apples for cooking, make sure you purchase lots for eating "out of hand" as well.*

Serves 4.

3	pounds chicken, cut into pieces
	No-salt seasoning
	Paprika
½	cup golden raisins
1	can (14 oz.) small boiled onions, drained
2	tart apples; peeled, seeded, and quartered
⅛	teaspoon cinnamon
	Pinch of cloves
1	tablespoon oat bran
1½	tablespoons flour
1	cup chicken stock
2	tablespoons crabapple (or apple) jelly

Preheat the oven to 300°. Remove the skin and all visible fat from the chicken. Arrange the chicken pieces in an oblong baking pan (breasts in the middle, thighs and legs on the ends). Sprinkle lightly with the no-salt seasoning and paprika. Plump the raisins for 2 to 3 minutes in boiling water, drain, and sprinkle over the chicken. Arrange the onions and apples over and around the chicken and raisins.

In a saucepan combine the cinnamon, cloves, oat bran, and flour. Slowly stir in the stock. Place the pan over medium-high heat and bring to a boil. Stir in the jelly and continue to stir until the jelly has melted and the liquid has thickened to a sauce-like consistency. Pour over the chicken. Cover the chicken tightly with heavy aluminum foil and bake for 1¾ hours.

Each serving provides:			
353	Calories	38 g	Carbohydrate
38 g	Protein	511 mg	Sodium
6 g	Fat	114 mg	Cholesterol

Chicken with Creamy Cucumber Dill Sauce

Cucumber and dill are one of the all-time great taste combinations, particularly in the summer. Serve this dish any time of year, but we recommend making it in midsummer when fresh dill is plentiful. It's a double treat to have enough to serve cold with the sauce for lunch the following day.

Serves 4.

2½-3   pounds chicken, cut into pieces, skin and all visible fat
       removed
¾   cup low-fat yogurt
1   large clove garlic, minced
2   teaspoons fresh parsley, minced
1   teaspoon fresh dill, chopped (¼ teaspoon if dried)
1   teaspoon fresh basil, minced (or ¼ teaspoon dried basil)
¼   teaspoon pepper
       No-stick vegetable oil spray

Place the chicken in a bowl and combine all of the remaining ingredients. Coat the chicken well with the marinade and let sit in the refrigerator for a minimum of 2 hours.

Coating

1   cup fine dry bread crumbs
½   cup Grape Nuts cereal, crushed
4   teaspoons fresh parsley, minced
½   teaspoon dried basil
½   teaspoon cumin
¼   teaspoon cayenne pepper

Combine all of the coating ingredients and spread on a plate. Dip the chicken pieces to coat well on all sides. Place the chicken in a shallow baking pan that has been sprayed with a no-stick vegetable oil spray. Bake in a preheated 350° oven for 1 hour. Serve with the following sauce on the side.

Each serving of chicken provides:			
362	Calories	34 g	Carbohydrate
39 g	Protein	416 mg	Sodium
7 g	Fat	109 mg	Cholesterol

Cucumber Dill Sauce

1   cup low-fat yogurt
1   clove garlic, minced
1   cup cucumber, peeled and grated (drain if watery)
2   teaspoons fresh dill, chopped (or ½ teaspoon dried)
1   teaspoon fresh lemon juice
2   pinches white pepper

Stir all of the sauce ingredients together and serve at room temperature as a side dish with the chicken.

Each serving of sauce provides:			
41	Calories	5 g	Carbohydrate
3 g	Protein	41 mg	Sodium
1 g	Fat	3 mg	Cholesterol

Chicken with Fresh Tomato and Dill Sauce

This is a nice dish to prepare in the summer when fresh dill and fresh tomatoes are abundant. Don't skimp on the dill.

Serves 4.

6	large tomatoes, peeled, seeded, and chopped
1	medium onion, chopped
⅓	cup celery, chopped
1	tablespoon fresh dill, minced
1	teaspoon lemon pepper
4	teaspoons sugar
1	tablespoon olive oil
2½	pounds chicken parts, skinned

Combine the tomatoes, onion, celery, dill, lemon pepper, and sugar in a medium-sized saucepan. Simmer over medium heat for 10 minutes. Heat the oil in a skillet and brown the chicken on both sides. Place in a casserole dish. Pour the sauce over the chicken pieces. Bake, uncovered, for 45 to 55 minutes, or until tender.

Each serving provides:

261	Calories	16 g	Carbohydrate
31 g	Protein	334 mg	Sodium
8 g	Fat	95 mg	Cholesterol

Parsley, Sage, Rosemary, and Thyme Chicken

Does this sound familiar . . . like a song title maybe? It's simple and delicious. The quantities of herbs listed below are for dried herbs. If you're able to get them fresh, the rule of thumb is 1 teaspoon dried equals 1 tablespoon fresh.

Serves 4.

2½-3 pounds chicken parts, skin and all visible fat removed
¼   cup lemon juice
2   tablespoons olive oil
1   small onion, chopped
1   teaspoon lemon pepper
3   tablespoons fresh parsley, finely chopped (or 1 tablespoon
           dried parsley flakes)
½   teaspoon celery seed
½   teaspoon rosemary
¼   teaspoon thyme
⅛   teaspoon sage

Arrange the chicken in a baking dish. Combine all of the remaining ingredients and pour over the chicken. Refrigerate for 3 hours. Bake in a preheated 350° oven for 1 hour.

Each serving provides:			
248	Calories	2 g	Carbohydrate
32 g	Protein	321 mg	Sodium
12 g	Fat	105 mg	Cholesterol

Chicken and Rice Casserole

This can be assembled in the morning and stored in the refrigerator until ready to bake — always a nice feature.

Serves 4 to 6.

1½	cups long grain rice, uncooked
	No-stick vegetable oil spray
2½-3	pounds chicken parts, skin and all visible fat removed
2	tablespoons oat bran
¾	teaspoon no-salt seasoning
2	tablespoons margarine
1	medium onion, chopped
2	cloves garlic, minced
1½	cups celery, chopped
1½	cans (15 oz.) beef broth
¾	cup water
¼	teaspoon freshly ground black pepper
½	teaspoon rosemary
½	teaspoon oregano

Toast the rice in a preheated 350° oven for 15 to 20 minutes, or until golden brown. Spray a large Teflon frying pan well with no-stick vegetable oil spray and sauté the chicken, sprinkling with the oat bran and no-salt seasoning as it browns. Remove the chicken to a warm plate and melt the margarine in the same pan. Add the onion and garlic and sauté until the onion is tender. Stir in all of the remaining ingredients, including the rice. Transfer to an 11 × 7-inch baking dish and arrange the chicken pieces in a single layer on top. Cover the dish *tightly* with aluminum foil. Bake in a preheated 350° oven for 50 minutes. If you like, sprinkle with freshly chopped parsley just before serving.

Note: If the casserole has just come out of the refrigerator, increase the baking time by 15 to 20 minutes.

Each serving provides:			
414	Calories	50 g	Carbohydrate
31 g	Protein	183 mg	Sodium
9 g	Fat	84 mg	Cholesterol

Chilean Chicken

This savory dish can be served at small dinner parties or at large buffets. If you're using a smaller amount of chicken, don't cut down on the amount of sauce. It's nice to have extra to serve at the table because it's so good!

Serves 8 to 10.

4-5	pounds chicken parts (about 15 pieces), skinned
3	tablespoons olive oil
1	medium onion, finely chopped
1	clove garlic, minced
½	green pepper, finely chopped
½	cup tomato paste
1	teaspoon basil
½	teaspoon rosemary
¼	teaspoon oregano
¼	teaspoon Tabasco sauce
2	tablespoons dry mustard
¼	cup Worcestershire sauce
½	cup honey
½	cup dry red wine

Brown the chicken pieces in 1½ tablespoons of the olive oil and place in a shallow baking pan, large enough to hold the chicken in a single layer; they should all get some of that good sauce. Combine all of the other ingredients (including the rest of the olive oil), except the red wine, in a saucepan.

Simmer the sauce for 20 minutes, stirring occasionally. Add the red wine and simmer for 15 minutes. Coat the chicken pieces with this sauce, cover with foil, and bake in a preheated 350° oven for 1 hour. Remove the foil and bake another 15 minutes, or until done. If making this a day ahead, brown the chicken pieces, add the sauce, and refrigerate overnight. The next day, bake as directed above.

Each serving provides:			
258	Calories	21 g	Carbohydrate
25 g	Protein	275 mg	Sodium
8 g	Fat	76 mg	Cholesterol

Curried Chicken

Long, slow cooking gives all of the flavors a chance to blend and produce a wonderfully tender and tasty chicken. The sauce is more like a broth and should be spooned over rice to really get the most out of this dish.

Serves 4.

1	tablespoon curry powder (Indian, if possible)
1	teaspoon powdered ginger
1	teaspoon minced garlic
¼	teaspoon crushed chili peppers
1	teaspoon turmeric
¼	teaspoon salt substitute
⅛	teaspoon nutmeg
⅛	teaspoon cinnamon
1	teaspoon sugar
1	tablespoon low-fat milk
2	medium onions, chopped
1	medium tomato, peeled, seeded, and chopped
1	small can (5½ oz.) low-fat evaporated milk
2	tablespoons plus 1 teaspoon flour
2½-3	pounds chicken parts, skinned and all visible fat removed

Mix the first nine ingredients together with the 1 tablespoon milk to form a paste. Add the onions and tomato. Shake the evaporated milk and flour in a small jar and when lump-free, pour into a small saucepan, and cook over medium heat, stirring constantly, until thickened.* Mix into the curry mixture. Place the chicken in a single layer in a shallow baking dish, and spoon the sauce over the top. Cover and bake in a preheated 250° oven for 3 hours. This curry can be made oven-ready in the morning or the night before.

*If you would like to skip this step, you can use Campbell's Cream of Mushroom Soup, Special Request.

Serve the curry with some (or all) of the following condiments on the table in small separate dishes: chopped bananas, coarsely chopped peanuts, plumped raisins (soaked in boiling water for 5 minutes), chopped green onions, and chutney.

Each serving provides:

269	Calories	15 g	Carbohydrate
37 g	Protein	167 mg	Sodium
6 g	Fat	112 mg	Cholesterol

Shawn's Cottage Pie

This is "comfort food" — and economical as well.

Serves 4 to 6.

1½   pounds ground chicken
      No-stick vegetable oil spray
1   medium onion, minced
1   large carrot, thinly sliced
      The following seasonings to taste: pepper, no-salt seasoning
        (or salt), oregano, onion powder, minced garlic
1   large celery stalk, minced
4   small to medium potatoes, peeled
¼-½ cup skim milk
      Paprika

Brown the chicken in a Teflon skillet that's been sprayed with the no-stick vegetable oil spray and drain. Add the onion, carrot, seasonings, and then the celery to the skillet. Cook, stirring occasionally, until the vegetables are tender-crisp. Transfer the chicken-vegetable mixture to a casserole that has been sprayed with no-stick vegetable oil spray. Boil the potatoes until soft. Whip with the skim milk, a little no-salt seasoning, and spread on top of the chicken mixture. Sprinkle with paprika and bake in a preheated 350° oven for 25 to 30 minutes, or until the top is nicely browned.

Each serving provides:			
316	Calories	24 g	Carbohydrate
27 g	Protein	133 mg	Sodium
12 g	Fat	113 mg	Cholesterol

Chicken with Rice and Vermicelli

A family dish that's tasty enough to serve to guests.

Serves 4.

½   cup uncooked vermicelli noodles, broken into small pieces
2   tablespoons olive oil
1   cup uncooked rice
3   cups onion, chopped
2½-3 pounds chicken parts, skin and all visible fat removed
    No-salt seasoning and pepper to taste
2   cups chicken stock

Sauté the vermicelli in 1 tablespoon of the olive oil until browned, stirring constantly (you want a medium brown color). Remove the vermicelli with a slotted spoon to a heavy casserole dish. Add the remaining 1 tablespoon oil to the oil remaining in the pan and brown the onions well. Wash the rice until the water runs clear, drain, and stir into the vermicelli. Place the chicken pieces on top and sprinkle with the no-salt seasoning and pepper. Spoon the browned onions over the chicken. Add the chicken stock. Cover *tightly* with a heavy lid or a double thickness of foil. Bake in a preheated 350° oven for 1 hour.

Each serving provides:			
516	Calories	57 g	Carbohydrate
40 g	Protein	148 mg	Sodium
13 g	Fat	105 mg	Cholesterol

Coq au Vin

Yes, you can make an honest to goodness Coq au Vin that is low in cholesterol! No fatty salt pork or butter in this version, but you and your guests won't even miss these traditional ingredients.

Serves 4.

4	tablespoons whole wheat flour
1	teaspoon no-salt seasoning
	Freshly ground black pepper to taste
2½-3	pounds chicken parts, skin and all visible fat removed
3	tablespoons safflower oil
1	can (14 to 16 oz.) miniature boiled onions, drained well
3	cloves garlic, minced
½	pound small whole mushrooms
2	cups dry red wine
1	bay leaf
⅛	teaspoon thyme
1	tablespoon fresh parsley, minced
1	teaspoon sugar
4-5	oz. lean ham slices, cut into narrow strips*

Place the flour in a paper or plastic bag and add the no-salt seasoning and freshly ground black pepper (roughly ¼ to ½ teaspoon). Shake the chicken pieces, one at a time, to coat. Heat the oil in a 10-inch skillet and brown the chicken pieces. Transfer the chicken to a small roasting pan or a large casserole dish. Add the onions.

*Look for ham that contains less than 5 percent fat.

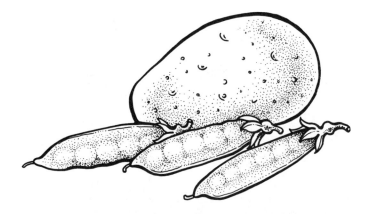

Add the garlic and mushrooms to the skillet and cook over medium heat for about 2 minutes. Remove from heat and stir in the flour remaining in the bag (there will be almost 3 tablespoons). Slowly stir in the wine. Add the bay leaf, thyme, parsley, and sugar. Return to heat and bring to a boil. Cook until sauce is reduced and thickened to the consistency of a cream sauce.

Sprinkle the ham strips over the top of the chicken, then pour on the sauce. Cover tightly and bake in a slow (250°) oven for 3 hours.

Each serving provides:

390	Calories	17 g	Carbohydrate
42 g	Protein	975 mg	Sodium
17 g	Fat*	120 mg	Cholesterol

---

*We know this looks high in fat, but it's actually a lower-fat version than the original — save it for special occasions.

Chicken Tourtière

Yes, it's possible to make a wonderful tourtière for your Christmas Eve supper — traditional in many homes, particularly those of French Canadian background. But, if you want it to taste like the real thing, you might have to relent and use that four-letter word S A L T, but not too much! And be sure to use our low cholesterol pastry (see page 257).

Serves 6.

1	pound ground chicken
¾	cup chicken stock
1	medium to large onion, finely chopped
¼	cup oat bran
2	cloves garlic, minced
¾	teaspoon thyme
¾	teaspoon oregano
¼	teaspoon ground allspice
¼	teaspoon ground cloves
¾	teaspoon salt (or half salt, half no-salt seasoning)
	Pastry for 2-crust pie
	Milk
	Lemon pepper

Mix together all of the ingredients, except the last three, in a larger, heavy-bottomed saucepan. Cook over low heat, stirring well about every 10 minutes, for 30 to 40 minutes. Let this cool, then place into a 9-inch pastry-lined pie plate and cover with the other half of the rolled-out pastry. Brush the pastry with the milk and sprinkle with the lemon pepper. Bake in a preheated 400° oven until the pastry is golden brown.

Serve accompanied by a nice tart jelly like cranberry jelly.

Each serving provides:			
634	Calories	55 g	Carbohydrate
21 g	Protein	530 mg	Sodium
37 g	Fat*	63 mg	Cholesterol

*We know this looks high in fat, but it's actually a lower-fat version than the original — save it for special occasions.

7

Stir-Fries and Other Oriental Specialties

STIR-FRY TIPS
(OR THE BEST WAY TO "WOK" YOUR CHICKEN)

Invest in a Chinese wok if you don't already have one. A wok uses less oil than a skillet. Remember to maintain a very high heat and to stir constantly for best results. If food starts to stick a bit (and this applies to sautéing as well), don't be tempted to add more oil — use a few drops of water instead.

Safflower oil and canola oil are fine for wok cooking, as are peanut oil, corn oil, and soybean oil. Olive oil, however, should be used only when cooking over low or medium heat. It's not recommended for using over the constant high heat needed for stir-frying.

Fresh ginger root adds a much better flavor than powdered ginger to stir-fried dishes. It can be kept in the freezer and grated as needed. Sesame oil, rice vinegar, hoisin sauce, and other oriental ingredients used frequently in the following recipes can be found in the imported foods section of many supermarkets.

Chicken and Vegetable Stir-Fry

The flavor of this dish is improved considerably by using fresh ginger root rather than powdered ginger. Serve over rice.

Serves 2 to 3.

½	pound boneless chicken breast
2	tablespoons fresh lemon juice
2	tablespoons safflower or canola oil
¼	teaspoon grated fresh ginger or pinch of powdered ginger
1	small green pepper, seeded and cut into long strips
1	small sweet red pepper, seeded and cut into long strips
3	green onions, cut into 1½-inch lengths
¼	pound snow peas
8	fresh mushrooms, cut into quarters
3	tablespoons cold water
1	tablespoon cornstarch
½	teaspoon sugar
2	tablespoons white wine

Skin the chicken breast and cut into long strips. Combine the lemon juice, oil, and ginger in a medium-sized bowl. Add the chicken strips, stir to coat, and marinate for 30 minutes to 1 hour. Clean the vegetables and cut into pieces as specified above. Place the water in a cup or small bowl; stir in the cornstarch, then the sugar, then the wine. Set aside until needed during the final stage of cooking.

Place a wok or large frying pan over high heat and add the chicken and marinade. Stir constantly until the chicken turns a whitish color; this will only take 2 to 3 minutes. As soon as the chicken looks cooked, stir in the green and red peppers, green onions, and snow peas. Continue to cook over high heat for an additional 3 minutes, stirring constantly. Stir in the mushrooms. Cook for another minute or two. With your spoon push the vegetables and chicken to sides of the wok and pour the cornstarch-water mixture into the center. Cook, stirring constantly, until this liquid boils and thickens. Stir the vegetables and chicken around in this mixture until coated. (Avoid overcooking the vegetables — tender-crisp and colorful vegetables are the sign of a good stir-fry!)

Each serving provides:			
227	Calories	12 g	Carbohydrate
20 g	Protein	55 mg	Sodium
10 g	Fat	44 mg	Cholesterol

Chicken and Broccoli Stir-Fry

Serves 4.

2   tablespoons safflower or canola oil
1   whole chicken breast, boned, skinned, and cut into cubes
1   medium sweet red pepper, cut into large pieces
4   green onions, chopped
2   cups broccoli flowerets
¼   cup dry sherry
2   tablespoons low-sodium soy sauce
2   tablespoons cornstarch
1   cup chicken stock

Heat the oil in a wok or large skillet over high heat. Cook the chicken for about 3 minutes, stirring constantly. Add the pepper, green onions, and broccoli. Stir-fry for 2 minutes. Add the sherry and soy sauce. Cover and cook for about 3 minutes, or until the vegetables are tender-crisp. Blend the cornstarch with the chicken stock, then stir into the wok. Cook, stirring constantly, for 2 minutes or until the sauce has thickened. Serve over hot, fluffy rice.

Each serving provides:			
204	Calories	12 g	Carbohydrate
17 g	Protein	370 mg	Sodium
8 g	Fat	34 mg	Cholesterol

David's Lemon Ginger Chicken Breasts

An inspiration of our friend David Brown, a Canadian actor, who can get a great meal together faster than anyone we know.

Serves 6.

2   lemons
1   inch piece of fresh ginger, grated
2   tablespoons safflower or canola oil
3   whole chicken breasts, boned, skinned, and cut into 1-inch
       strips
1   small can (4 oz.) red pimientos, drained and diced

Combine the juice of the 2 lemons, the grated rind of 1 lemon, the ginger, and the oil. Place the chicken breasts in this marinade and let sit for about 2 hours (although it can sit all day if refrigerated). Stir-fry everything gently, except the pimiento, for roughly 3 to 5 minutes, or until the chicken is cooked through. Sprinkle the pimientos over the chicken for the last minute or two of cooking and serve the chicken with the pan juices.

Each serving provides:			
178	Calories	2 g	Carbohydrate
27 g	Protein	82 mg	Sodium
6 g	Fat	68 mg	Cholesterol

Stir-Fry Garden Vegetables

This really stretches out a small amount of leftover chicken.

Serves 4 to 6.

1	tablespoon safflower oil
1	clove garlic, minced
1	medium onion, thinly sliced
3	small zucchini, cut into ½ × 2-inch strips
15-20	snow peas
1	green pepper, cut into thin strips
1	red pepper, cut into thin strips
½	pound fresh mushrooms, thinly sliced
1	cup cooked chicken, diced
½	cup water chestnuts, sliced
2	large tomatoes, cut into wedges

Sauce

¼	cup low-sodium soy sauce
⅓	cup honey
3	tablespoons water
1	tablespoon cornstarch
2	tablespoons lemon juice
½	teaspoon fresh ginger, grated (or ¼ teaspoon powdered)

Once the stir-frying has started, it requires full attention. Combine all of the sauce ingredients and set aside. The vegetables should also be prepared before the actual cooking begins. Cut the vegetables uniformly thin and place in individual bowls in order of use: garlic, onion, zucchini, snow peas, green pepper, red pepper, mushrooms, sauce, chicken, water chestnuts, and tomatoes.

Put the wok on a supporting ring over high heat. Flick a few drops of water onto the surface. When the drops dance, add the oil by pouring it around the rim so the wok's sides are evenly coated. Add the vegetables in the order listed, stir-frying each for approximately 1 minute. The idea is to keep the vegetables in constant motion so that they are lightly cooked very quickly. The best utensil, with a little practice, is a pair of long, slender chopsticks. When the mushrooms are lightly cooked, add the sauce, chicken, and water chestnuts. Cover the wok, remove from heat, and grasping both the wok handle and the cover handle, shake to coat the vegetables with the sauce. Return to heat, add the tomatoes, and stir. Spoon the vegetables and chicken into a shallow serving dish and serve immediately with hot, fluffy rice.

Each serving provides:			
247	Calories	41 g	Carbohydrate
12 g	Protein	519 mg	Sodium
5 g	Fat	25 mg	Cholesterol

Ginger Chicken Stir-Fry

Serves 4.

Sauce

2   tablespoons low-sodium soy sauce
2   tablespoons hoisin sauce
2   tablespoons cornstarch
1   teaspoon grated fresh ginger
¼   teaspoon Louisiana hot sauce

1   whole chicken breast, skinned and boned
1   tablespoon safflower or canola oil
2   small cloves garlic, crushed
        No-salt seasoning
1   green pepper, seeded and cut into cubes
1   small bunch green onions, trimmed and cut into 2-inch
          lengths
2   medium carrots, thinly sliced on the diagonal
1¼   cups (10 oz.) chicken stock
¼   pound fresh snow peas, trimmed
1   can (10 oz.) sliced mushrooms, drained
1   can (10 oz.) whole water chestnuts, drained and cut in half

Combine the sauce ingredients and set aside. Slice the chicken meat into bite-size strips. Heat the oil in a wok or large skillet. Add the garlic and chicken and stir-fry over high heat for 2 minutes. Sprinkle with the no-salt seasoning. Add the green pepper, green onions, and carrots. Stir-fry for an additional 3 minutes. Add the chicken stock and snow peas. Cover and cook for 3 minutes. Add the sauce ingredients along with the mushrooms and water chestnuts. Bring to a boil, stirring constantly, and let boil for 1 minute, or until the sauce has thickened but the vegetables are still tender-crisp. Serve immediately over hot rice.

Each serving provides:			
219	Calories	26 g	Carbohydrate
18 g	Protein	804 mg	Sodium
5 g	Fat	34 mg	Cholesterol

Hot Chinese Salad

A friend calls this dish our "chop suey" salad. It's easy and excellent.

Serves 6.

2	whole chicken breasts, skinned, boned, and cut into 1-inch pieces
¼	cup cornstarch
2	tablespoons canola or safflower oil
¼	teaspoon garlic powder
1	can (10 oz.) sliced water chestnuts, drained
1	can (10 oz.) sliced mushrooms, drained
1	large tomato, cut into chunks
1	bunch green onions, cut into 2-inch pieces
1	cup celery, sliced diagonally
¼	cup low-sodium soy sauce
2	cups finely shredded iceberg lettuce

Roll the chicken in the cornstarch. Heat the oil in a wok or large skillet over high heat. Add the chicken pieces and brown. Sprinkle with the garlic powder. Add the water chestnuts, mushrooms, tomato, green onions, and celery and stir. Add the soy sauce and stir. Cover and reduce heat to simmer. Cook for 5 minutes. Lightly toss the chicken and vegetable mixture with the lettuce and serve at once. Some hot, fluffy rice would round out the meal.

Each serving provides:			
200	Calories	17 g	Carbohydrate
21 g	Protein	587 mg	Sodium
6 g	Fat	46 mg	Cholesterol

Spicy Orange Chicken Stir-Fry

The combination of spicy hot peppers and a refreshing, zesty orange flavor make this a great-tasting dish.

Serves 2.

1	large whole chicken breast (½ pound), boned and skinned
4	green onions, sliced diagonally into ½-inch pieces
2	tablespoons dry sherry
2	tablespoons low-sodium soy sauce
1	teaspoon fresh ginger, grated
1	clove garlic, minced
¼	teaspoon crushed red pepper flakes
½	cup orange juice
1¾	teaspoons cornstarch
	Grated peel of 1 orange
1	tablespoon sesame oil

Cut the chicken breasts into small strips (about ¼ inch × 2 inches). Combine the green onions, sherry, soy sauce, ginger, garlic, and crushed red pepper in a bowl just large enough to hold the chicken. Toss the chicken in the mixture and marinate for at least 20 to 30 minutes.

Combine the orange juice, cornstarch, and orange peel. Set aside.

In a wok or large skillet, heat the sesame oil. Drain the chicken but reserve the marinade. Stir-fry the chicken for about 2 minutes over high heat. Stir the remaining marinade into the orange juice mixture. Pour over the chicken and stir-fry until the sauce thickens.

Serve over rice. This is also nice served on a bed of lightly sautéed fresh bean sprouts and julienned red and green peppers.

Each serving provides:			
306	Calories	15 g	Carbohydrate
36 g	Protein	700 mg	Sodium
9 g	Fat	86 mg	Cholesterol

Chicken Egg Rolls

Chinese egg rolls are often high in cholesterol. Here's a satisfying version that tastes "forbidden" but is strictly low-fat.

Makes 30 egg rolls.

2½	cups cabbage, finely shredded
2	cups bean sprouts
1½	cups cooked chicken, chopped
½	cup onion, chopped
½	cup celery, chopped
1	can (10 oz.) sliced mushrooms, drained
1	tablespoon safflower or canola oil
¾	teaspoon black pepper
3	tablespoons low-sodium soy sauce
30	large wonton skins
	No-stick vegetable oil spray

Combine all of the ingredients (except the egg roll skins) in a mixing bowl. Place 2 tablespoons of the filling in the center of an egg roll skin. Moisten two sides and one end of the skin with water. Fold over one moistened edge past the center. Fold the opposite edge over the top and seal by pressing down gently. Fold in the ends to make a packet and seal by pressing down. Place the completed rolls on a cookie sheet lightly sprayed with a no-stick vegetable oil spray. Lightly spray the top and sides of the rolls with the oil. At this point, the rolls may be covered tightly with foil and refrigerated or frozen.

If the rolls are frozen, let them thaw at room temperature. When thawed, bake in a preheated 400° oven for 10 minutes. Turn the rolls over and bake for an additional 4 to 5 minutes. Serve with plum sauce* for dipping.

*Prepared plum sauce can be found in the imported foods section of many supermarkets.

Each serving provides:			
67	Calories	10 g	Carbohydrate
4 g	Protein	95 mg	Sodium
1 g	Fat	6 mg	Cholesterol

Sesame Thigh Stir-Fry

This stir-fry is definitely addicting, but we wouldn't suggest making it for a crowd. It can get tiresome cutting out the bits of fat and boning the thighs, although you could do this a day ahead. Save the bones for low-salt soup or stock.

Serves 3 (or 2 with large appetites).

1½	pounds chicken thighs
2	tablespoons low-sodium soy sauce
2	teaspoons sesame oil
2	tablespoons lemon juice
2	teaspoons brown sugar
1	clove garlic, minced
4	drops Louisiana hot sauce
1	tablespoon canola oil
1	cup zucchini, diced
1	cup celery, diced
1	cup fresh mushrooms, diced
1	teaspoon cornstarch

To bone the thighs, start with the end that has the thicker bone, and with a small sharp knife, work your way along the bone with a scraping motion toward the small end. Skin, remove all visible fat, and cut the meat into strips or bite-size squares. Combine the soy sauce, sesame oil, lemon juice, brown sugar, garlic, and hot sauce. Place the chicken in the marinade and let sit for 30 minutes to 1 hour.

Heat the canola oil in a wok or large skillet and stir-fry the zucchini, celery, and mushrooms until tender-crisp (add the mushrooms a minute or two after the celery and zucchini). Remove the vegetables with a slotted spoon to a warm plate. Drain the chicken, reserving the marinade. Add the chicken to the wok and stir-fry over high heat until cooked through, stirring and flipping the pieces to separate them. Stir the cornstarch into the reserved marinade and add to the wok along with the cooked vegetables. Let boil up to thicken, stirring constantly. Serve with fluffy white rice.

Each serving provides:			
265	Calories	10 g	Carbohydrate
28 g	Protein	556 mg	Sodium
13 g	Fat*	108 mg	Cholesterol

*Although this is mostly the "good" type of fat, you may want to save this recipe for a special occasion.

Chris Bishop's Szechwan Chicken in Lettuce Cups

Serves 4.

2   whole chicken breasts, skinned, boned, and cut into ½-inch
        strips
2   tablespoons cornstarch
2   tablespoons low-sodium soy sauce
2   egg whites
4   cloves garlic, minced
½   teaspoon crushed red pepper flakes
1   head iceberg lettuce
¼   cup canola or safflower oil
½   cup slivered almonds
2   small red or yellow bell peppers, cut into strips

Combine the chicken breasts with the cornstarch, soy sauce, egg whites, garlic, and crushed red pepper. Marinate for 3 hours in the refrigerator. Prepare the Ginger Sauce below and set aside.

Two or 3 hours before dinner, prepare the lettuce by cutting the core out of the head and gently separating the leaves. Rinse under cold running water. Drain, place in a plastic bag lined with paper towels, and store in the refrigerator.

When ready to cook, heat the oil in a wok and stir-fry the nuts for 2 minutes, or until golden. Remove with a slotted spoon and set aside.

Drain the chicken. Discard any remaining marinade. Stir-fry the chicken for 2 minutes in the wok over high heat. Add the bell peppers. Add the Ginger Sauce and cook just until the sauce boils. Add the nuts. Serve at room temperature accompanied by a bowl of lettuce leaves. Let each guest spoon some chicken mixture onto a chilled leaf, roll up, and eat.

Ginger Sauce

¼   cup low-sodium soy sauce
¼   cup red wine
2   tablespoons dry sherry
2   tablespoons rice vinegar
1   tablespoon honey
½   teaspoon fresh ginger, finely chopped

Mix all of the sauce ingredients together in a small bowl.

Each serving provides:			
431	Calories	17 g	Carbohydrate
34 g	Protein	928 mg	Sodium
24 g	Fat*	68 mg	Cholesterol

*We know this looks high in fat, but it's actually a lower-fat version than the original — save it for special occasions.

Thai Noodles and Chicken

A hot and spicy dish that's perfect for four, or two people who want leftovers. And they will . . . they'll want an early lunch!

Serves 4.

1½	teaspoons cornstarch
4	teaspoons dry sherry
1	teaspoon sesame oil
¼	teaspoon fresh ginger, grated
1	clove garlic, minced
1	pound boneless, skinless chicken breasts
1	small bunch green onions, trimmed and cut into 2-inch pieces
1	small zucchini, julienned
1	small sweet red pepper, julienned
2	tablespoons olive oil
1	pound linguini, cooked

Combine the first five ingredients in a small bowl. Cut the chicken into thin strips and add to the bowl. Mix, cover, and let sit in the refrigerator for about 1 hour. Place the chopped vegetables in a plastic bag or covered bowl and let sit in the refrigerator until ready to cook. Meanwhile, make the following sauce.

When ready to assemble the dish, heat 2 tablespoons of olive oil in a wok or skillet. Drain the chicken and stir-fry until no trace of pink remains (about 3 minutes). Add the vegetables to the wok and continue to stir-fry until the vegetables are tender-crisp (about 2 to 3 minutes). Add the sauce. Stir well and when heated through, pour over hot, cooked linguini. Toss well to coat the noodles.

Note: Toasted sesame seeds sprinkled on top of the noodles make a very attractive garnish.

Sauce

1	cup chicken stock
1	tablespoon low-sodium soy sauce
2	tablespoons tomato paste
1	teaspoon crushed red pepper flakes
1½	teaspoons sugar
1½	teaspoons sesame oil
1½	tablespoons cornstarch
1½	tablespoons cold water

Combine all of the ingredients (except the cornstarch and water) in a small saucepan. Stir over medium heat until hot. Dissolve the cornstarch in the water and add to the sauce. Cook, stirring constantly, until the sauce is thick and clear. (This sauce can be made ahead and reheated.)

Each serving provides:			
631	Calories	96 g	Carbohydrate
43 g	Protein	313 mg	Sodium
7 g	Fat	66 mg	Cholesterol

Mu Shu Chicken

These are really tasty — great party fare. Don't be spooked by making your own pancakes; they might sound complicated, but they're really quite simple. As an alternative, perhaps your neighborhood Chinese restaurant would sell you some for a special occasion. If you make your own, you may want to make them ahead and store them in the freezer. They freeze very well.

Serves 8 to 10 (2 to 3 pancakes per person).

Pancakes

3¼   cups flour
¼   cup green onions, sliced very thinly
1   cup boiling water
⅓   cup cold water
       No-stick vegetable oil spray

Stir together 3 cups of the flour and the onions. Slowly add the boiling water, stirring until well blended. Stir in the cold water. As soon as the dough is cool enough to handle, turn out onto a floured surface. Work in the remaining ¼ cup flour, kneading about 8 to 10 minutes, or until the dough is elastic and smooth. Shape the dough into a ball. Place in a bowl, cover, and let stand for 15 to 20 minutes.

Turn the dough out onto a lightly floured surface. Divide the dough in half. Form each half into a 12-inch-long roll. Cut each roll into 1-inch pieces. Flatten each piece with the palm of your hand. Using a rolling pin, roll each piece into a 6½- to 7-inch circle. Spray the entire surface of one side of each pancake lightly with the no-stick vegetable oil spray. Stack the pancakes in twos, sprayed sides together.

In a large Teflon pan, cook the pancake stacks, 1 or 2 stacks at a time, over medium heat, for 30 to 40 seconds, or until bubbles appear on the underside. Turn each stack and cook for an additional 30 to 40 seconds. Quickly remove from the pan and gently separate the two pancakes. Let cool.

Stack the cooled pancakes, separating each with wax paper. To store: Wrap the entire stack in foil and refrigerate or freeze.

To use: Thaw the pancakes at room temperature. Remove the wax paper from between the pancakes and rewrap in the foil. Heat in a preheated 375° oven for 8 to 10 minutes.

Makes 24 pancakes.

Filling

2	whole chicken breasts, skinned and boned
1	clove garlic, minced
2	tablespoons safflower or canola oil
3	cups Chinese cabbage (or regular cabbage), shredded
2	cups carrots, julienned (about 2 inches long)
1	package (6 oz.) snow peas, (thawed if frozen)
1	small can (8 oz.) water chestnuts, drained and sliced
½	cup green onions, chopped
⅓	cup low-sodium soy sauce
2	tablespoons dry sherry
2	teaspoons cornstarch
½	teaspoon powdered ginger
¼	teaspoon black pepper

Cut the chicken into thin strips and stir-fry with the garlic in the hot oil until the chicken is no longer pink (about 3 minutes). Don't overcook. Add the cabbage, carrots, snow peas, water chestnuts, and green onions. Stir-fry for an additional 2 minutes. In a small bowl, combine the soy sauce, sherry, cornstarch, ginger, and pepper. Add to the wok and cook, stirring constantly, until thickened. Spoon the hot filling into the warmed pancakes and roll up. This recipe makes enough filling for 24 pancakes.

Each serving (per filled pancake) provides:			
118	Calories	17 g	Carbohydrate
7 g	Protein	151 mg	Sodium
2 g	Fat	11 mg	Cholesterol

Chicken Pot Stickers

Pot stickers are an increasingly popular appetizer. They're delicious but usually high in fat. With a little experimenting, we've been able to produce a low-fat version that looks authentic and tastes wonderful.
                              Serves 6 (about 6 pot stickers per person).

1	cup green cabbage, finely shredded
4	tablespoons white wine
1	pound ground chicken
4	teaspoons low-sodium soy sauce
2	cloves garlic, minced
1-2	inch length of fresh ginger, peeled and grated or finely chopped
1	green onion, finely chopped
1	teaspoon sesame oil
1	teaspoon sugar
40	wonton skins
1	teaspoon cornstarch mixed with 1 teaspoon water
2	tablespoons sesame oil
1-2	cups chicken stock

Combine the cabbage, white wine, ground chicken, soy sauce, garlic, ginger, green onion, 1 teaspoon sesame oil, and sugar in a large bowl and mix well (hands do the best job). Take 1 teaspoon of the mixture and place on a wonton skin (keep the unused skins under a damp cloth while you work). Fold each wonton skin over and seal with the cornstarch and water mixture. You may have to pleat the top of the wonton to make a small compact package. Flatten the bottom of the dumpling slightly. Continue this process until you have used up all of the filling.

Heat the 2 tablespoons of sesame oil in a skillet. Fry the dumplings, about 10 to 12 at a time, on their flattened bottoms until their bottoms are brown and crispy (about 3 to 4 minutes).

In another saucepan containing about ½ inch of the chicken stock, steam the browned dumplings for about 3 minutes with the lid on. Return to the skillet for 3 to 5 minutes to finish "crisping." (They'll be soft on top and crispy on the bottom.) Serve with the following sauce for dipping.

Makes 40 dumplings.

Dipping Sauce

¼   cup low-sodium soy sauce
2   tablespoons rice vinegar
1   teaspoon sesame oil

Combine all of the ingredients in a small bowl. Mix well.

Each pot sticker provides:			
61	Calories	7 g	Carbohydrate
4 g	Protein	94 mg	Sodium
2 g	Fat	9 mg	Cholesterol

8

Chicken and Pasta Dishes

Pasta is no longer a trend — it is a classic — and it is here to stay. Including a pasta section in this book, then, was a definite must.

We all know by now that pasta is more than spaghetti, right? Pasta comes in rings, shells, spirals, strands, elbows, tubes, and even moustache shapes. We have tried to give a good cross-section in this chapter. Along with recipes for the more familiar dishes, such as spaghetti, lasagne, tetrazzini, and cacciatore, we offer some really exciting sauces for linguini.

Pasta is one of the few foods where fresh does not necessarily mean best. A good quality, golden-colored commercial dried pasta made with 100 percent semolina flour from durum wheat is a better product than an inferior, pale-colored fresh one that can sometimes cook too quickly and become gummy. While we frequently buy fresh pasta (making sure it is not matted or clumped together), we also keep boxes of dried pasta in the pantry. Keep one or two in your cupboard and you will never be stuck for an emergency meal — particularly if you have one of our good sauces in the refrigerator or freezer to combine it with.

Red Pepper, Fresh Mushroom, Dill, and Chicken Pasta Sauce

The low-fat evaporated milk gives this sauce the creamy texture so typical of many delicious pasta sauces but without the calories and fat.

Serves 4.

2	cloves garlic, minced
½	cup onion, diced
2	tablespoons safflower or canola oil
2-3	cups fresh mushrooms, sliced
1	tablespoon fresh dill, chopped
1	large red pepper, seeded and julienned
¾	cup low-fat evaporated milk
3	tablespoons flour
¾	cup chicken stock
½	teaspoon pepper
2	cups cooked chicken, diced
1	pound pasta, cooked

In a large skillet, sauté the garlic and onions in the oil. Add the mushrooms, dill, and red pepper. Cook until the vegetables are tender-crisp. Shake the evaporated milk and flour together in a small jar. Add to the vegetable mixture with the chicken stock and pepper, and simmer gently until the sauce thickens. Stir in the chicken. Serve over your favorite cooked pasta.

Each serving provides:			
709	Calories	100 g	Carbohydrate
41 g	Protein	131 mg	Sodium
15 g	Fat	70 mg	Cholesterol

Spaghetti with Chicken Balls

Served with a tossed green salad, a crusty loaf of bread, and a good bottle of dry Italian red wine, this pasta dish makes a fine Italian-style meal.

Serves 4.

1   pound spaghetti

Spaghetti Sauce

1   cup onion, diced
1   large can (28 oz.) tomatoes, mashed
1   can (14 oz.) tomato sauce
1   can (10 oz.) sliced mushrooms, undrained
2   teaspoons sugar
1   teaspoon basil
1   teaspoon oregano
2   teaspoons fresh parsley, minced
½   teaspoon pepper

Combine all of the above ingredients in a large saucepan. Bring to a boil. Reduce heat to simmer and cook slowly, covered, for 20 minutes. Add the meatballs just before serving.

Chicken Balls

2   tablespoons bread crumbs
2   tablespoons oat bran
½   teaspoon celery seed
½   teaspoon thyme
½   teaspoon black pepper
1   tablespoon Parmesan cheese
1   large clove garlic, minced
¼   cup onion, finely chopped
¼   cup green pepper, finely chopped
1   pound ground chicken
      No-stick vegetable oil spray

Mix the dry ingredients in a large bowl. Add all of the remaining ingredients, except the chicken, mixing well. Blend in the ground chicken and form into 12 to 16 balls. Spray a cookie sheet with the no-stick vegetable oil spray. Bake the chicken balls in a preheated 350° oven for 15 to 20 minutes.

Cook spaghetti in 3 quarts of boiling water, uncovered, until *al dente* (about 7 to 12 minutes). Drain and arrange on a warm platter. Spoon the sauce and chicken balls over the spaghetti.

Each serving provides:			
738	Calories	114 g	Carbohydrate
41 g	Protein	1,356 mg	Sodium
14 g	Fat	95 mg	Cholesterol

D and G Sun-Dried Tomato Pasta

This recipe was invented by actor David Brown and bridge player Genni Macaulay especially for this book. It might seem like a lot of oil, but olive oil is monounsaturated and this makes 3 to 4 servings. The recipe is so quick and so good, we just had to include it.

Serves 3 to 4.

4	tablespoons olive oil
1	whole (½ to ¾ pound) chicken breast, skinned and boned
½	teaspoon lemon pepper
½	clove garlic, minced (or ⅛-¼ teaspoon garlic powder)
¼	cup sun-dried tomatoes
1	tablespoon minced fresh basil (or ½ teaspoon dried)
1	teaspoon grated fresh lemon rind
¾	pound fresh linguini*
¼	cup grated Parmesan cheese

Heat 2 tablespoons of the olive oil in a medium-sized skillet. Cut the chicken breast into strips (about ¼ to ½ inch wide). Sprinkle with the lemon pepper and garlic. Sauté the chicken until cooked through (about 2 to 3 minutes on each side). Remove the chicken to a warm, covered dish.

Soak the sun-dried tomatoes in boiling water for 2 to 3 minutes (if you're using the type marinated in oil, eliminate this step). Cut the tomatoes into slivers. Cook the linguini. Add the tomatoes, chicken, remaining 2 tablespoons of olive oil, basil, and lemon rind to the cooked linguini and toss. Add the Parmesan cheese and toss again.

This is delicious served hot or at room temperature.

*Dry linguini (enough for 3 to 4 people) may be substituted for fresh, or try one of the thinner noodles such as spaghettini or angel hair pasta.

Each serving provides:			
605	Calories	67 g	Carbohydrate
31 g	Protein	335 mg	Sodium
24 g	Fat*	124 mg	Cholesterol

*Although this is mostly the "good" type of fat, you may want to save this recipe for a special occasion.

Make Ahead Chicken Cacciatore and Pasta

A green salad with Italian dressing and garlic bread would be great accompaniments.

Serves 4 to 6.

2½-3 pounds chicken parts, skinned
3   tablespoons flour
½   teaspoon no-salt seasoning
½   teaspoon black pepper
2   tablespoons olive oil
1   medium onion, chopped
1   clove garlic, minced
1   large can (28 oz.) tomatoes, broken up with a fork
1   small can (7½ oz.) tomato sauce
½   teaspoon basil
½   teaspoon oregano
1   tablespoon fresh parsley, chopped
1   pound pasta, cooked

Wash the chicken under cold running water. Remove all visible fat and dry well with paper towels. Shake the chicken pieces in the flour mixed with the no-salt seasoning and pepper. (A brown paper lunch bag does this job nicely.) Heat the olive oil in a Dutch oven and brown the chicken lightly. Add the onion and garlic and let brown slightly. Add all of the remaining ingredients (make sure the sauce covers all of the chicken pieces). Simmer, uncovered, until the chicken is tender (50 to 60 minutes). Do not stir, but give the pot a couple of gentle shakes from time to time to make sure the chicken is not sticking. When done, remove from heat. Cover and allow to sit for several hours or overnight in the refrigerator. (This allows the flavors to blend.) Reheat at serving time. Serve over the cooked pasta.

Each serving provides:			
598	Calories	83 g	Carbohydrate
40 g	Protein	616 mg	Sodium
11 g	Fat	84 mg	Cholesterol

Tangy Chicken Drumsticks and Pasta

For healthy hearts and hearty appetites. (These drumsticks freeze well. Divide into individual servings with the cooked pasta and store in the freezer.)

Serves 4 to 5.

1	medium onion, chopped
2	teaspoons olive oil
1	clove garlic, minced (or 1 teaspoon garlic powder)
1	can (14 oz.) tomatoes, undrained
2	tablespoons apple cider vinegar
2	tablespoons molasses
1	tablespoon prepared mustard
½	teaspoon chili powder
⅛	teaspoon cayenne pepper
8-10	chicken drumsticks, skinned
1	pound linguini or spaghetti, cooked

Sauté the onion in the olive oil in a medium-sized saucepan until soft. Add the garlic, tomatoes (break them up with a fork), vinegar, molasses, mustard, chili powder, and cayenne. Cook over medium-low heat, uncovered, for 30 minutes, or until the mixture has thickened slightly. Cool slightly, then pour into a blender or food processor and process until smooth. Place the drumsticks in a shallow baking pan in a single layer and spoon the sauce on top. Cover and bake in a preheated 350° oven for 45 minutes. Remove the cover and bake for an additional 45 minutes. Place the drumsticks on top of hot, cooked pasta on individual serving plates and spoon the sauce over the top.

Each serving provides:			
648	Calories	99 g	Carbohydrate
42 g	Protein	333 mg	Sodium
9 g	Fat	95 mg	Cholesterol

Creamy Paprika Balls with Linguini

Serves 4.

1	pound ground chicken breast
¼	cup bread crumbs
½	teaspoon lemon pepper
1	clove garlic, minced
	No-stick vegetable oil spray
1	cup onions, finely sliced
1¼	cups chicken stock
¾	cup low-fat evaporated milk
¼	cup flour
1	tablespoon paprika
1	teaspoon lemon pepper
1	pound linguini, cooked
2	tablespoons fresh parsley, minced

Combine the chicken, bread crumbs, lemon pepper, and garlic. Shape into about 16 small balls. Spray a cookie sheet with the no-stick vegetable oil spray and put the balls on the cookie sheet. Bake for 15 minutes in a preheated 350° oven.

Sauce directions: Spray a skillet with the no-stick vegetable oil spray and lightly sauté the onions. Add the chicken stock. Combine the evaporated milk and flour, blending well, and stir into the stock and onions. Cook slowly, stirring constantly, until smooth and thickened. Stir in the paprika and lemon pepper, then add the chicken balls. Serve over hot linguini. Sprinkle with the minced parsley.

Each serving provides:			
675	Calories	105 g	Carbohydrate
47 g	Protein	498 mg	Sodium
6 g	Fat	74 mg	Cholesterol

Marilyn's Linguini

Did you know that jalapeño peppers are thought to be helpful in protecting against heart disease? They are thought to stimulate the mechanism that dissolves blood clots.

Serves 4.

2	teaspoons fermented black beans*
1	pound boneless, skinless chicken breasts
½	teaspoon no-salt seasoning
4	tablespoons olive oil
4	tablespoons oyster sauce*
2	jalapeño peppers, seeded and cut into slivers
2	cloves garlic, minced
12	oz. fresh linguini (or equivalent in dried), cooked
2	tablespoons chopped fresh cilantro sprigs (or parsley)

Blanch the fermented black beans in boiling water for 20 seconds, then rinse with cold water and set aside.

Cut the chicken breasts into strips (¼ to ½ inch wide) and sprinkle with the no-salt seasoning. Heat the oil in a skillet and sauté the chicken breasts for 2 to 3 minutes on each side, or until *almost* cooked. Add the oyster sauce, fermented black beans, jalapeño peppers, and garlic. Continue to sauté until the peppers start to wilt. Toss well with the cooked linguini. Garnish with the cilantro leaves.

Note: You can cook the linguini ahead of time (until *al dente*), rinse in cold water, refrigerate, then combine with the chicken and peppers just before serving. Place in a preheated 400° oven for 2 to 3 minutes to make sure everything is heated through. Then enjoy!

*If the fermented black beans and oyster sauce aren't available at your supermarket, try stores specializing in Asian foods, or ask your favorite Chinese restaurant where they buy theirs.

Each serving provides:			
519	Calories	51 g	Carbohydrate
39 g	Protein	885 mg	Sodium
17 g	Fat	166 mg	Cholesterol

Oriental Chicken Stir-Fry with Linguini

One whole chicken breast can be stretched into four adult servings, making this dish pleasing to your budget as well as your palate.

Serves 4.

1	whole chicken breast, skinned and boned
1	tablespoon safflower oil
½	teaspoon lemon pepper
4	green onions, cut into 1-inch pieces
2	cups zucchini, cut into 2-inch strips
1	large carrot, thinly sliced on the diagonal
1	sweet red pepper, cut into 1-inch pieces
2	cups mushrooms, cut into halves or quarters
2¼	cups chicken stock
1	pound linguini, cooked

Sauce

2	tablespoons low-sodium soy sauce
2	tablespoons hoisin sauce
2	tablespoons cornstarch
1	teaspoon sesame oil
1	teaspoon powdered ginger

Cut the chicken into bite-size strips. Heat the oil in a wok or large skillet. Add the chicken strips and sprinkle with the lemon pepper. Stir-fry over high heat for 2 minutes. Add all the vegetables, except the mushrooms, and stir-fry for an additional 3 minutes. Add the chicken stock, cover, and cook for 3 minutes.

Combine all of the sauce ingredients, stir until smooth, then add to the wok along with the mushrooms. Bring to a boil, stirring constantly, and let boil for 1 minute or until thick and glossy looking. Serve immediately over the hot linguini while the vegetables are still tender-crisp.

Each serving provides:

606	Calories	100 g	Carbohydrate
32 g	Protein	732 mg	Sodium
8 g	Fat	34 mg	Cholesterol

Chicken Rigatoni

Serves 4.

2	cloves garlic, minced
½	cup onion, diced
1	green pepper, chopped
2	tablespoons olive oil
1	can (19 oz.) crushed tomatoes
1	teaspoon oregano
1	teaspoon basil
1½	teaspoons garlic powder
½	teaspoon pepper
2	cups cooked chicken breast meat, diced
2	cups rigatoni pasta (4 cups cooked)

Sauté the onion, garlic, and green pepper in the oil until soft. Add all of the remaining ingredients, except the chicken and pasta. Simmer, uncovered, for 20 to 30 minutes. (The sauce will reduce and thicken.) Add the chicken. Toss with the cooked rigatoni or place the rigatoni in a large serving dish and spoon the sauce over the top.

Each serving provides:			
419	Calories	49 g	Carbohydrate
31 g	Protein	275 mg	Sodium
11 g	Fat	60 mg	Cholesterol

Six Vegetables Chicken Pasta

A dish with six vegetables has to be good for you, right?

Serves 6 to 8.

4	whole chicken breasts, boned, skinned, and cut into thin strips
2	tablespoons safflower or canola oil
1	clove garlic, minced
½	cup onion, diced
½	green pepper, seeded and julienned
2	cups fresh mushrooms, sliced
2	cups fresh broccoli flowerets
2	carrots, julienned
3	tablespoons flour
1	teaspoon lemon pepper
1½	cups low-fat evaporated milk
6-8	cups cooked spiral-shaped pasta
	Freshly grated Parmesan cheese (optional)

In a large skillet, gently sauté the chicken strips in the oil until just cooked (chicken will lose its pinkish color). Add the garlic, onion, and all of the vegetables. Cook until tender-crisp. Sprinkle the flour over the chicken and vegetables and stir to coat. Add the lemon pepper. Stir in the milk and combine well. Simmer until the sauce thickens. Serve over hot pasta.

Have a bowl of freshly grated Parmesan cheese on the table for people to sprinkle over the top of the pasta if they wish.

Each serving provides:			
436	Calories	52 g	Carbohydrate
39 g	Protein	243 mg	Sodium
7 g	Fat	76 mg	Cholesterol

Chicken Tetrazzini

Serves 6.

1	pound thin spaghetti
	No-stick vegetable oil spray
1	whole chicken breast, cooked,* skinned, and boned
2	tablespoons soft margarine
1	small onion, chopped
¼	cup green pepper, chopped
2	tablespoons flour
1	teaspoon instant chicken bouillon powder
1	teaspoon dry mustard
1	teaspoon lemon pepper
1	can (10 oz.) sliced mushrooms, drained, but reserve liquid
1	can (14 oz.) low-fat evaporated milk
¼	cup dry sherry
1	cup low-fat mozzarella cheese, grated
2	tablespoons Parmesan cheese (optional)
2	tablespoons fresh parsley, chopped

Cook the spaghetti according to package directions. Drain and rinse with cold water. Drain again and place in a 9 × 13-inch baking dish that's been sprayed with a no-stick vegetable oil spray. Cut the cooked chicken into thin strips and place over the spaghetti.

Melt the margarine in a large saucepan and sauté the onion and green pepper until soft. Stir in the flour, chicken bouillon powder, dry mustard, and lemon pepper. Add the reserved mushroom liquid to a measuring cup and add enough water to make 1½ cups. Slowly stir this into the saucepan along with the evaporated milk and sherry (a whisk is good for this). Cook, stirring constantly, over medium-high heat until the sauce comes to a boil. Stir, while boiling, for 1 minute. Stir in the mushrooms. The sauce should be

*See Best Ever Method for Cooking Chicken Breasts (page 18). Or 3 cups cooked leftover poultry may be substituted for the chicken breasts. It's a great way to use up some of that leftover Christmas turkey.

the consistency of a very *thin* cream sauce. (It might seem a little soupy, but the pasta will absorb the moisture.) Pour the sauce over the chicken and spaghetti. Sprinkle with the cheese. Bake in a preheated 350° oven for 20 to 25 minutes, or until bubbly and golden. Sprinkle the parsley over the top just before serving.

Each serving provides:			
502	Calories	70 g	Carbohydrate
30 g	Protein	804 mg	Sodium
9 g	Fat	41 mg	Cholesterol

Three Pepper Pasta

This dish also makes a nice pasta salad for summer entertaining when served cold. When serving as a salad use a thin noodle, such as vermicelli.

Serves 4.

1	(roughly ¾ pound) skinless, boneless chicken breast
½	teaspoon no-salt seasoning
3	tablespoons olive oil
2	small cloves garlic, minced
	Generous sprinkling of freshly ground black pepper
⅓	teaspoon oregano
⅓	teaspoon basil
	Pinch of crushed red pepper flakes
4	medium bell peppers (1 yellow, 2 red, 1 green), thinly sliced
3	tablespoons red wine vinegar
12	oz. linguini, spaghetti, vermicelli, or fusilli pasta, cooked

Cut the chicken breast into strips about ¼ to ½ inch wide. Sprinkle with the no-salt seasoning. Heat 2 tablespoons of the olive oil in a large skillet. Sauté the chicken breasts for 2 to 3 minutes on each side, or until cooked through. Set aside and keep warm. Add the remaining 1 tablespoon oil to the skillet along with the garlic, black pepper, herbs, and crushed red pepper. Stir over high heat for 1 minute. Add the sliced bell peppers and sauté, stirring frequently, for about 5 minutes. (You want the peppers cooked, but not too wilted.) Remove from heat and stir in the red wine vinegar. Add the cooked chicken strips and toss with the cooked pasta.

Each serving provides:			
492	Calories	68 g	Carbohydrate
31 g	Protein	64 mg	Sodium
10 g	Fat	49 mg	Cholesterol

Chicken with Pasta, Yogurt, and Sun-Dried Tomatoes

We're sure any food lover will agree that sun-dried tomatoes are a great taste sensation. They combine very well with the chicken, yogurt, chili sauce, and garlic.

Serves 3.

¾	cup sun-dried tomatoes
2	cups spiral-shaped pasta
1	cup cooked chicken, diced
¼	cup sliced black olives (optional)
½	cup low-fat yogurt
2	tablespoons mild, red chili sauce
1	clove garlic, minced
½	teaspoon freshly ground black pepper

Soak the sun-dried tomatoes in boiling water for 2 to 3 minutes to soften. (Skip this step if you're using the kind marinated in olive oil.) Drain, cut into slivers, and place in a large bowl with the hot pasta, chicken, and olives. Combine the yogurt, chili sauce, garlic, and black pepper. Add to the bowl of pasta and toss. Serve warm. (You can reheat in a 325° oven for about 10 minutes if necessary.)

Each serving provides:			
444	Calories	39 g	Carbohydrate
21 g	Protein	1,514 mg	Sodium
23 g	Fat*	44 mg	Cholesterol

*Although this is mostly the "good" type of fat, you may want to save this recipe for a special occasion.

Chicken Lasagne

You'll never miss the beef (or the fat) in our chicken version of this classic Italian favorite. One of our guests said it ranked right up with the best he'd ever eaten. Bring out the red checkered tablecloth, toss up a Caesar salad, warm up a loaf of crusty Italian bread, decant a good, robust Chianti, and enjoy!

Serves 6 to 8.

2	tablespoons olive oil
1	medium onion, chopped
2	cloves garlic, minced (or 1½ teaspoons garlic powder)
1½-2	pounds ground chicken
1	teaspoon lemon pepper
½	teaspoon salt or no-salt seasoning
1	teaspoon oregano
½	teaspoon basil
1	can (28 oz.) tomatoes
1	can (5½ oz.) tomato paste
1	tablespoon fresh parsley, minced (or 1 teaspoon parsley flakes)
¼	teaspoon chili powder
½	teaspoon sugar
½	large green pepper, seeded and diced
9	lasagne noodles (cooked according to package directions)
1	cup low-fat ricotta or cottage cheese
1¼	cups low-fat mozzarella cheese, grated
2	tablespoons Parmesan cheese

Heat the olive oil in a large skillet. Sauté the onions and garlic until soft. Add the chicken and cook, stirring frequently, until no trace of pink remains. Sprinkle with the lemon pepper, salt, oregano, and basil. Remove from heat. Place the tomatoes, tomato paste, parsley, chili powder, and sugar in a food processor (or blender) and blend just enough to mash the tomatoes. Add to the chicken mixture along with the green pepper and simmer the sauce for 20 minutes.

To assemble: Spread 1 cup of the sauce in the bottom of a 9 ×
13-inch baking dish (the sauce does not need to cover the bottom
completely). Place 3 cooked noodles on top and spread ⅓ of the
remaining sauce over the noodles. Dot with half of the ricotta or
cottage cheese. Sprinkle with ½ cup of the mozzarella cheese.
Place 3 more noodles on top of the cheese. Spread another ⅓ of
the sauce on top, dot with the remaining ricotta or cottage cheese,
and sprinkle with ½ cup mozzarella cheese. Place the last 3 noodles on top. Spread with the remaining sauce and sprinkle with
the Parmesan cheese and the remaining mozzarella. Bake, uncovered, in a preheated 350° oven for 30 minutes.

Each serving provides:			
455	Calories	37 g	Carbohydrate
36 g	Protein	1,057 mg	Sodium
18 g	Fat*	104 mg	Cholesterol

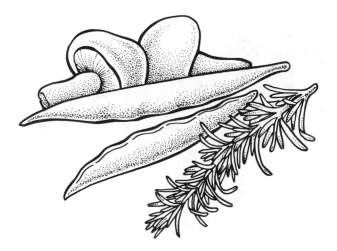

*We know this looks high in fat, but it's actually a lower-fat version than
the original — save it for special occasions.

Chicken Manicotti

If you can find the type of cannelloni shell made with egg whites, which doesn't need boiling (Catelli makes them), they would be perfect for this dish. It's so much easier to stuff a stable cylinder than a cooked, floppy one.

Serves 6 to 8.

12-16 manicotti shells (or cannelloni shells)

Filling

1½	cups cooked chicken breast meat, chopped
½	cup onion, finely chopped
¼	cup parsley, chopped
¼	teaspoon ground thyme
½	cup celery, finely chopped (or fresh mushrooms)
1	clove garlic, minced
1	cup low-fat mozzarella cheese, grated
¼	cup dry white wine
½	teaspoon pepper (or to taste)

Combine the filling ingredients, adding the pepper to taste.

Sauce

2	tablespoons soft margarine
2	tablespoons all-purpose flour
1	cup chicken stock
1	cup low-fat milk
¼	cup grated Parmesan cheese
½	teaspoon nutmeg

In a medium saucepan, melt the margarine and stir in the flour. Gradually stir in the chicken stock and milk, stirring constantly over medium heat until the mixture thickens. Stir in the Parmesan cheese and nutmeg.

Cook the pasta shells according to package directions. Drain the shells, rinse with cold water, and stuff immediately with the filling. Cover the bottom of a 9 × 13-inch baking pan with 1 cup of sauce. Arrange the filled shells in single layer and spoon any remaining sauce on top. Cover with foil and bake in a preheated 350° oven for 45 minutes to 1 hour.

Note: This dish can be prepared early in the day and refrigerated until just before baking time. It's a great party dish.

Each serving provides:			
256	Calories	24 g	Carbohydrate
20 g	Protein	293 mg	Sodium
8 g	Fat	37 mg	Cholesterol

Spaghetti with Sauce

Serves 3.

1	tablespoon olive oil
1	medium onion, chopped
1	large clove garlic, minced
1	cup fresh mushrooms, sliced
1	can (14 oz.) peeled tomatoes
3	tablespoons tomato paste
1	tablespoon fresh parsley, minced (or 1½ teaspoons dried parsley)
½	teaspoon oregano
½	teaspoon honey
⅛	teaspoon freshly ground black pepper
½	teaspoon no-salt seasoning
1	cup cooked chicken, diced
½	pound spaghetti, cooked

Heat the olive oil in a medium saucepan with a heavy bottom. Sauté the onion over high heat for 1 to 2 minutes, then add the garlic and mushrooms. Turn heat to low and continue to cook until the onions and mushrooms are tender, stirring frequently. (If they seem to be sticking to the pan, add a tiny bit of water or wine, but let it evaporate before adding the rest of the ingredients.) Add all of the remaining ingredients, except the chicken. Bring to a boil. Cover, reduce heat to simmer, and cook for 30 minutes, stirring occasionally to break up tomato pieces. Add the chicken and heat for several minutes. Toss with hot spaghetti.

Each serving provides:			
472	Calories	70 g	Carbohydrate
26 g	Protein	393 mg	Sodium
10 g	Fat	42 mg	Cholesterol

Spaghetti with Sauce, Bolognese Style

If you have just a little bit of leftover chicken and are in a pasta mood, this sauce is perfect!

Serves 2.

	No-stick olive oil spray
½	cup onion, chopped
1	large clove garlic, minced
1	cup fresh mushrooms, sliced
2	tablespoons white wine
1	can (7½ oz.) tomato sauce
½	teaspoon Italian seasoning*
¼	teaspoon sugar
	Freshly ground black pepper to taste
½	cup cooked chicken, diced
¼	pound spaghetti, cooked

Spray a medium-sized Teflon skillet with the no-stick olive oil spray. Sauté the onion, garlic, and mushrooms for about 3 minutes, stirring frequently. Add the wine and let boil up, stirring occasionally, until the wine has evaporated. Add all of the remaining ingredients and simmer for 3 to 5 minutes, stirring occasionally. Serve over hot spaghetti.

*If you have no Italian seasoning on hand, substitute basil.

Each serving provides:			
348	Calories	56 g	Carbohydrate
20 g	Protein	685 mg	Sodium
4 g	Fat	31 mg	Cholesterol

9

Fun Food and Some Great Recipes for Leftover Chicken

High cholesterol is not a condition found only in the middle age and older group. It's found in younger people as well. And what dishes do teenagers and young adults enjoy? Burritos, fajitas, pizza pops and quesadillas must surely be among their favorites. In this chapter you'll find recipes for these, as well as for fondue, crêpes, and more.

Many of the recipes, you'll see, call for precooked chicken. For these, leftover chicken works just fine. And in all of the recipes using precooked chicken, leftover turkey can be substituted with equally good results. Chapters 2, 7, and 8 also have some excellent recipes for leftover chicken.

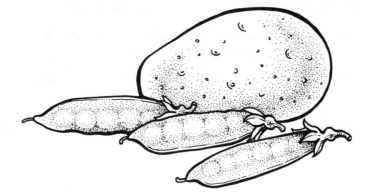

Great Chicken Curry

Serves 6.

1	large onion
3	cloves garlic, minced
1-2	tablespoons olive oil
2	rounded tablespoons curry powder
1	tablespoon cumin
1	teaspoon hot mixed spices*
2	cups chicken stock
1	cup tomato sauce (or 2 tablespoons tomato paste)
1	cup fresh mushrooms, sliced (or 10 oz. canned mushrooms, drained)
1	sweet red pepper, chopped
3-4	cups cooked chicken, diced
1	small Red Delicious apple, chopped
2	tablespoons flour
2	tablespoons sherry
6	large prunes, pitted and chopped
	Salt (or no-salt seasoning) and pepper to taste

Cut the onion into 4 wedges, then slice. In a Dutch oven or large heavy-bottomed pot, sauté the onion and garlic in the oil. Add the curry, cumin, hot mixed spices, chicken stock, tomato sauce, mushrooms, red pepper, and chicken. Simmer *very* gently for about 20 minutes. Add the apple and simmer for an additional 10 minutes. Combine the flour and sherry and add to the curry along with the prunes. Simmer for 5 more minutes and add the salt and pepper to taste. Serve with rice and some or all of the following condiments: chutney, chopped bananas, and raisins.

*Any store that sells Indian spices should have the hot mixed spices. If you can't find any, substitute ¼ teaspoon ginger and ⅛ teaspoon cayennepepper.

Each serving provides:			
295	Calories	22 g	Carbohydrate
27 g	Protein	449 mg	Sodium
11 g	Fat	73 mg	Cholesterol

Jeff's Chicken Burritos

Eleanor's son Jeff created these for one of our many chicken testing dinners, and they were a great hit. Our eight children and their spouses were a tremendous help with this book. We'll never again refer to them as our "little chickens."

Serves 8 to 10.

1	pound chicken breasts, skinned, boned, and all visible fat removed
1	tablespoon safflower or canola oil
1	large onion, finely chopped
2	large cloves garlic, minced
2	tablespoons flour
2	teaspoons chili powder
1	teaspoon cumin
½	cup chicken stock
1	cup buttermilk
1	can (4 oz.) chopped green chilies, drained (not jalapeño peppers)
1	tablespoon tomato paste
1	package flour tortillas

Cut the chicken into ¼-inch strips. Heat the oil in a 10-inch skillet and add the chicken. Sauté the chicken until no longer pink, about 2 to 3 minutes. Remove the chicken to a plate or bowl. In the same skillet, sauté the onion and garlic until soft, about 3 minutes. Mix in the flour, chili powder, and cumin, stirring constantly, until well blended. Gradually stir in the chicken stock, buttermilk, chilies, and tomato paste. Simmer, stirring constantly, until slightly thickened. Stir the chicken into the sauce. Remove from heat and cool slightly.

Place about ¾ cup of this filling on the lower third of each flour tortilla and roll up. Place seam-side down in an ungreased, shallow 9 × 13-inch baking pan and bake in a preheated 350° oven until heated through (about 10 minutes).

Burritos are traditionally served with guacamole and sour cream. Avocados are high in fat, but it's monounsaturated and so quite acceptable unless you are counting calories. If you must use sour cream, use low-fat, or better yet, use yogurt.

	Each serving provides:		
217	Calories	30 g	Carbohydrate
17 g	Protein	371 mg	Sodium
3 g	Fat	30 mg	Cholesterol

Chicken Fajitas

Fajitas are tasty and great for entertaining. Place the wrapped warm tortillas in the center of the table and the hot skillet on a hot pad next to them. Let everyone fill and wrap their own tortillas. We like to place dishes of fresh chopped tomatoes, salsa,* guacamole, chopped green onions, and yogurt on the table as well.

Serves 3 to 4.

1	pound boneless, skinless chicken breasts, cut into 2-inch strips
2	tablespoons olive oil
½	large green pepper, cut into thin strips
½	large red pepper, cut into thin strips
1	large mild onion, cut into wedges, then into thin slices *lengthwise*
6	flour tortillas, warmed (see recipe instructions)

Marinade

½	cup water
¼	cup low-sodium soy sauce
2	large cloves garlic, smashed
2	teaspoons fresh ginger, peeled and diced
2	tablespoons brown sugar
2	tablespoons lime juice (bottled is fine)
1	tablespoon cornstarch
1	teaspoon onion powder
½	teaspoon coriander
¼	teaspoon cumin

To make the marinade, put the water, soy sauce, garlic, and ginger in a blender and puree. Add the remaining marinade ingredients. Pour over the chicken strips and marinate for 1 hour.

*Check out our salsa recipes on pages 261 and 262.

When ready to cook, heat 1 tablespoon of the olive oil in a heavy-bottomed skillet. Drain the chicken well, reserving ¼ cup of the marinade. Sauté the chicken in the oil for 2 to 3 minutes. Add the peppers and onion and continue to cook, stirring, for an additional 2 to 3 minutes or until the vegetables are tender-crisp. Chicken should be just about cooked by this time. Just before serving, boil the reserved marinade and pour into the skillet, and drizzle with the other 1 tablespoon of the olive oil. Place under a preheated broiler for 1 to 2 minutes. Serve piping hot.

Note: To warm the tortillas, wrap them in a damp kitchen towel and place in a 200° oven for about 20 minutes.

Each serving provides:			
581	Calories	72 g	Carbohydrate
45 g	Protein	1,331 mg	Sodium
12 g	Fat	88 mg	Cholesterol

Chicken Fondue

Fondues are great fun. One pot won't accommodate more than four people because the broth cools off too quickly with too many people dipping pieces of cold chicken into the pot. Fondue is an intimate way to share a meal with that special person! Proper long-handled fondue forks are needed to spear the dunkables and put them into the hot broth. Some sets come with different colored handles so that diners can keep track of their own forks. These forks, however, will be too hot to put into your mouth, so you should have regular forks for eating. We've seen special fondue plates with sections to hold a variety of sauces, but these are not essential.

Serves 4.

2½   cups chicken stock
        Dash of ground ginger
2   pounds chicken breasts, boned, skinned, and cut into
           1-inch cubes*
½   pound fresh whole mushrooms (brush to clean — do not
           wash)
½   head cauliflower, cut into flowerets
1½-2 cups broccoli flowerets
2   small zucchini, cut into chunks

Heat the stock and ginger in a fondue pot. Bring to a boil and keep over constant heat. Each diner spears the chicken cubes and assorted raw vegetables and cooks to desired "doneness" in the boiling broth. Serve with sauces of your choice.

Note: The above vegetables are good choices because they don't require too much cooking and are at their best when tender-crisp. Asparagus would also be a good choice.

*Don't cut the chicken cubes thicker than 1 inch or they won't cook through.

Each serving provides:			
225	Calories	11 g	Carbohydrate
40 g	Protein	137 mg	Sodium
3 g	Fat	86 mg	Cholesterol

Chicken Pizza Pops

Great fare for watching the Super Bowl, the World Series, or . . . anything!

Makes 8 Pizza Pops.

1	loaf frozen bread dough
2	whole chicken breasts, skinned, boned, and halved
1-2	tablespoons safflower or canola oil
½	cup hot salsa
⅓	cup low-fat mozzarella cheese, grated

Thaw the frozen dough and cut into 8 pieces. Cut each half breast into 2 pieces. In a medium-sized frying pan, sauté the chicken lightly in oil until the chicken loses its pinkish color. Don't overcook — you want the chicken just firm to the touch. Roll each section of dough out on a floured surface. Roll the pieces of dough large enough so that each chicken piece fits onto half. Put a chicken piece on each piece of dough and top with the salsa and cheese. Fold over and seal the edges with water. To make sure the salsa and cheese end up in equal amounts in each Pizza Pop, we like to roll all the pieces of dough, set all the chicken on the dough, and then portion out the salsa and cheese.

Allow to rise 30 minutes, then bake in a preheated 400° oven for 15 minutes. Serve with extra salsa on the side.

Each serving provides:

254	Calories	28 g	Carbohydrate
19 g	Protein	442 mg	Sodium
7 g	Fat	39 mg	Cholesterol

Chicken Quesadillas

When purchasing tortillas for this recipe, make sure you get the flour rather than the corn tortillas. The amounts given are per person, so you can make quesadillas for one or two, or for a crowd.

Serves 1.

¼	cup cooked chicken breast meat, shredded
1	slice mild onion, separated into rings
⅓	cup low-fat mozzarella cheese, shredded
1	tablespoon canned green chilies, chopped and seeded
1	flour tortilla
2	teaspoons grated Parmesan cheese
	No-stick vegetable oil spray

Place the chicken, onion, mozzarella cheese, and chilies over one half of the tortilla to within ½ inch of the edge and sprinkle with the Parmesan. Fold the tortilla over and spray both sides with the no-stick vegetable oil spray. Broil about 3 inches from heat until the top is lightly browned (about 2 minutes). Turn over and brown the other side. The cheese should be melted and the filling well heated through by this point. If you prefer your quesadilla spicier, spoon 1 tablespoon salsa over it after cooking.

Each serving provides:

287	Calories	27 g	Carbohydrate
26 g	Protein	710 mg	Sodium
7 g	Fat	48 mg	Cholesterol

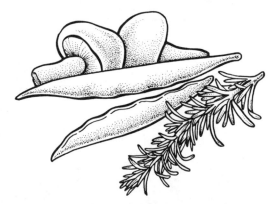

Chili with Leftover Chicken

An unusual way to use leftover chicken, it's also very economical. And who doesn't love chili?

Serves 6.

1	large onion, chopped
1	tablespoon olive oil
2	cans (14 oz. each) tomato sauce
2½	tablespoons chili powder
2	cans (14 oz. each) kidney beans, undrained
1	clove garlic, minced (or 1 teaspoon garlic powder)
1	teaspoon onion powder
½	teaspoon lemon pepper
½	teaspoon oregano
½	teaspoon chili peppers
1	can (14 oz.) tomatoes, undrained (break up with a fork)
1-1½	cups cooked chicken, diced

In a Dutch oven or large heavy-bottomed pot sauté the onion in the olive oil until soft. Add all of the remaining ingredients and simmer, uncovered, for 30 minutes.

Each serving provides:			
259	Calories	36 g	Carbohydrate
18 g	Protein	1,493 mg	Sodium
6 g	Fat	26 mg	Cholesterol

Chicken Enchiladas

Serves 4 to 6.

1	tablespoon olive oil
1	onion, chopped
1	clove garlic, minced
6	mushrooms, sliced
½	green pepper, chopped
1½	cups cooked kidney beans
1	can (14 oz.) stewed tomatoes
1	tablespoon chili powder
1	teaspoon ground cumin
½	cup red wine
	No-salt seasoning (or salt) to taste
1	whole cooked chicken breast, skinned, boned, and cubed
8	corn tortillas
	No-stick vegetable oil spray
1½	cups grated low-fat mozzarella cheese
1	cup ricotta cheese and ½ cup low-fat yogurt, blended together

In a large skillet, heat the olive oil and sauté the onion, garlic, mushrooms, and green pepper until soft. Add the beans, tomatoes, chili powder, cumin, and wine. Add the no-salt seasoning to taste. Simmer, uncovered, for 30 minutes. (Sauce will reduce and thicken.) Stir in the chicken. Put a layer of 4 tortillas in an 8-inch square baking dish that has been sprayed with the no-stick vegetable oil spray. Top with half of the sauce, 3 tablespoons of the mozzarella cheese, and 3 tablespoons of the ricotta and yogurt mixture. Place the remaining tortillas on top of this layer and spread with the remaining sauce. Spoon the remaining yogurt mixture over this and sprinkle with the rest of the mozzarella cheese. Bake for 15 to 20 minutes in a preheated 350° oven.

Each serving provides:			
453	Calories	47 g	Carbohydrate
36 g	Protein	697 mg	Sodium
15 g	Fat	58 mg	Cholesterol

Louisiana Peppers

This recipe, the result of an attempt to come up with something different for leftover poultry (including that Thanksgiving turkey), was a hit. Red peppers were slightly more popular than green. Comments ranged from "good, but too spicy" (grandmother) and "not spicy enough" (father), to "hey! great Mom!" (teenagers).

Serves 4.

4	large bell peppers (red or green)
1	package Spanish Rice A Roni (or Spanish Minute Rice)
1	can (19 oz.) tomatoes, drained and chopped
2	cups cooked chicken, chopped
1	large clove garlic, minced
3	green onions, sliced
¼	cup fresh parsley, chopped
2	good pinches cayenne pepper
1½	tablespoons Louisiana hot sauce
	Sprinkling of salt and pepper

Slice the peppers lengthwise and remove the seeds. Cook the Rice A Roni according to package directions but use the 19 oz. can of tomatoes. When the rice is cooked, fold in all of the remaining ingredients. Stuff the peppers and place in a baking dish. Cover with a lid or foil and bake in a preheated 350° oven for 40 minutes, or until the peppers are soft.

Each serving provides:			
414	Calories	47 g	Carbohydrate
28 g	Protein	1,526 mg	Sodium
13 g	Fat	62 mg	Cholesterol

Coach Wheel Chicken Pie

The following recipe is a particularly good way of dealing with that leftover Christmas turkey.

Serves 4 to 6.

1	cup carrots, sliced
1	cup cut green beans
2	cups chicken stock
1	can or jar (14 oz.) whole onions, save liquid
¼	cup flour
2	cups cooked chicken (or turkey), diced
½	teaspoon thyme (or summer savory)
½	teaspoon barbecue spice
¼	teaspoon powdered ginger

Simmer the carrots and green beans in the chicken stock until fork-tender. Pour the reserved onion liquid into a jar, add the flour, and shake until smooth. Add this liquid to the vegetables and stock along with all of the remaining ingredients. Simmer until well heated through. Pour into an 8-inch square baking dish. Arrange the following biscuits on top and bake in a preheated 450° oven for 10 to 12 minutes. Reduce heat to 350° and continue to bake until the biscuits are done (about 8 to 10 minutes).

Biscuits

2	cups flour
½	teaspoon salt
4	teaspoons baking powder
⅔	cup milk
¼	cup safflower oil
1	cup low-fat mozzarella cheese, grated
3	teaspoons fresh parsley, minced (or 1 teaspoon dried parsley)

Sift the flour, salt, and baking powder into a bowl. Combine the milk and oil and stir into the flour mixture with a fork until the dough forms a ball. Knead five to ten times. Roll into a rectangle about ½ inch thick. Sprinkle with the grated cheese and parsley flakes. Roll up from the long side and slice into 9 pieces, roughly ½ inch thick. Place on top of the chicken mixture and bake. The chicken mixture should be hot when the raw biscuits are placed on top. If it has cooled, put in the oven until the edges are bubbly, then arrange the biscuits gently over the top.

Each serving provides:			
523	Calories	54 g	Carbohydrate
31 g	Protein	1,150 mg	Sodium
20 g	Fat*	62 mg	Cholesterol

*Although this is mostly the "good" type of fat, you may want to save this recipe for a special occasion.

Chicken Pot Pie with Biscuits

A wonderful way to serve leftover chicken. Keep it in mind during the holiday season as well; it doubles nicely and would make a welcome change from all of the rich food that abounds that time of year.

Serves 3 to 4.

2	cups chicken stock
2	teaspoons fresh parsley, chopped
½	cup cut green beans
1	small potato, peeled and diced
½	cup celery, diced
1	cup carrots, sliced
½	cup peas
3	tablespoons flour
¼	cup water
¼	teaspoon lemon pepper
1½-2	cups cooked chicken, cubed

Put the chicken stock into a pot and add the parsley and all of the vegetables, except the peas. Cook until tender. Add the peas. Shake the flour, water, and lemon pepper in a small jar and add to the pot, stirring until the mixture thickens. Stir in the chicken. Remove from heat and spoon into an 8-inch square baking dish. Top with the following biscuit dough and bake in a preheated 450° oven for 10 to 12 minutes. Reduce heat to 350° and continue baking until the biscuits are done (about 8 to 10 minutes).

Biscuits

2	cups flour
½	teaspoon salt
2	teaspoons baking powder
¼	cup safflower oil
⅔	cup low-fat milk

Stir together the dry ingredients. With a fork, stir in the oil and milk until the dough forms a ball. Knead gently five to ten times. Roll or pat out to about ½ inch thick on a floured surface and cut into rounds or wedges. Place gently over the chicken mixture and bake immediately as directed above.

Each serving provides:

585	Calories	67 g	Carbohydrate
30 g	Protein	664 mg	Sodium
21 g	Fat	60 mg	Cholesterol

Spanish Fricassee

Serve this spicy fricassee over rice.

Serves 2.

2	tablespoons olive oil
½	cup onion, coarsely chopped
¼	cup green pepper, diced
1	small clove garlic, crushed
1-1½	teaspoons chili powder
½	teaspoon cumin
1½	cups cooked chicken, cut into small chunks
½	cup chicken stock
1	can (14 oz.) whole tomatoes (don't drain but break up tomatoes with a fork)
2	tablespoons olives, chopped

In a 12-inch skillet, heat the oil and add the onion, green pepper, garlic, chili powder, and cumin. Cook about 4 minutes, stirring frequently, until the onions are translucent. Add the chicken. Cook and stir 2 minutes. Stir in the stock and tomatoes. Bring to a boil. Cover the skillet and simmer, stirring occasionally, for 30 to 35 minutes. Add the olives and simmer an additional 5 minutes, uncovered. If you want the sauce to reduce a bit more, cook uncovered until it reaches the desired consistency, but make sure there is enough liquid to flavor the rice.

Each serving provides:

401	Calories	14 g	Carbohydrate
34 g	Protein	649 mg	Sodium
24 g	Fat*	93 mg	Cholesterol

---

*Although this is mostly the "good" type of fat, you may want to save this recipe for a special occasion.

Chicken Stroganoff

Serves 6.

2	tablespoons soft margarine
1	medium onion, thinly sliced and separated into rings
2	cups fresh mushrooms, sliced
3	tablespoons flour
2½	cups chicken stock
1½	tablespoons tomato paste
1	teaspoon paprika
½	teaspoon basil
⅛	teaspoon nutmeg
3	tablespoons sherry
2½-3	cups cooked chicken, cut into thin strips
¾	cup low-fat yogurt
6-8	cups egg noodles, cooked

Melt 1 tablespoon of the margarine in a 12-inch skillet. Add the onion, then the mushrooms, and cook over medium heat until soft (about 5 minutes). Remove the onion and mushrooms to a small mixing bowl. Melt the remaining margarine in the skillet and stir in the flour. Continue to stir until the flour is golden brown. Whisk in the stock, tomato paste, paprika, basil, nutmeg, and sherry. Simmer until thickened (about 10 minutes). Stir in the chicken, onions, and mushrooms. Simmer until well heated through. Stir in the yogurt just before serving. Serve immediately over hot noodles.

Each serving provides:			
396	Calories	41 g	Carbohydrate
28 g	Protein	192 mg	Sodium
12 g	Fat	101 mg	Cholesterol

Chicken and Broccoli Crêpes

Crêpes can turn leftover chicken into an elegant meal.

Serves 4.

2	tablespoons soft margarine
½	cup onion, chopped
2	tablespoons flour
1	cup low-fat milk
½	teaspoon no-salt seasoning
¼	teaspoon grated lemon rind
¼	teaspoon lemon pepper
2	tablespoons reduced-calorie mayonnaise
4	cups cooked chicken breast meat, diced
1½	cups tiny broccoli flowerets, steamed until tender-crisp
	No-stick vegetable oil spray

Melt the margarine in a saucepan and sauté the onion until soft. Sprinkle the flour over the onion and stir until absorbed. Gradually stir in the milk and cook, stirring constantly, until thickened. Stir in the no-salt seasoning, lemon rind, and lemon pepper. Remove from heat and whisk in the mayonnaise. Stir in the chicken and broccoli. Let cool, and prepare the crêpes.

Low-Fat Crêpes

2	egg whites
1½	cups low-fat milk
1	cup sifted flour
	Pinch of salt
2	teaspoons safflower or canola oil

In a bowl, lightly beat together the egg whites and milk. Whisk in the flour and salt until smooth. Cover the batter and refrigerate for 1 hour. Lightly brush a 6-inch no-stick crêpe or omelette pan with the oil. Heat over medium-high heat. Stir the batter. Lift the pan from heat and pour in about 2 tablespoons batter per crêpe, swirling the pan so that the batter covers the bottom thinly. Cook until set and the edges are dry — this should only take about 1 minute. Lift carefully with a spatula and turn over gently, or grasp the crêpe with the fingers of both hands and turn to cook the other side for about 20 to 30 seconds.

To store the crêpes, put wax paper between each one, stack them, and wrap the stack in foil. Store in the refrigerator until needed.

Makes 8 crêpes.

To assemble: Spoon 2 to 3 tablespoons of the filling in the center of each crêpe and roll up. Place in a shallow baking pan that has been sprayed with the no-stick vegetable oil spray and bake in a preheated 350° oven for 10 to 15 minutes. This makes enough for 8 crêpes, or 2 per person.

Optional: Each crêpe may be sprinkled with 1 to 2 teaspoons grated low-fat mozzarella cheese about halfway through baking.

Each serving provides:			
422	Calories	34 g	Carbohydrate
37 g	Protein	349 mg	Sodium
15 g	Fat	79 mg	Cholesterol

Asparagus Chicken Crêpes

You'll need 8 crêpes (see the Low-Fat Crêpe recipe on page 246).

Serves 4.

½	cup red onion, chopped
1½	cups fresh mushrooms, sliced (or canned mushrooms, drained)
2	tablespoons safflower or canola oil
2	tablespoons flour
⅔	cup chicken stock
½	cup low-fat evaporated milk
2	cups cooked chicken breast meat, diced
2	cups fresh asparagus, chopped and steamed until tender-crisp
2	tablespoons Parmesan cheese
1	teaspoon lemon pepper
8	crêpes
	No-stick vegetable oil spray
¼	cup low-fat mozzarella cheese, grated

In a small skillet, lightly sauté the onion and mushrooms in the oil. Stir in the flour until the onion and mushrooms are coated. Gradually stir in the stock and milk, stirring constantly until the sauce has thickened. Stir in the chicken, asparagus, Parmesan, and lemon pepper. Place 2 to 3 tablespoons of the filling on each crêpe, roll up, and place on a 9 × 13-inch baking dish or cookie sheet that has been sprayed with the no-stick vegetable oil spray. Sprinkle with the mozzarella cheese. Bake in a preheated 350° oven for 15 minutes, or until well heated through.

Each serving provides:			
464	Calories	40 g	Carbohydrate
39 g	Protein	479 mg	Sodium
16 g	Fat	73 mg	Cholesterol

Curried Chicken Crêpes

See the recipe for Low-Fat Crêpes in this chapter, page 246.

Serves 4 (2 crêpes each).

½	cup celery, minced
½	cup onion, minced
2	tablespoons soft margarine
3	tablespoons flour
1	teaspoon curry powder
1	cup chicken stock*
½	cup tomato juice
2	cups cooked chicken breast meat, diced
1½	teaspoons lemon pepper
8	crêpes
	No-stick vegetable oil spray

Sauté celery and onion in the margarine until soft. Stir in the flour and curry powder. Add the stock and tomato juice and cook, stirring constantly, until thickened. Add the chicken and lemon pepper. Let cool. Spoon 2 to 3 tablespoons of the filling onto each crêpe, roll up, and place on a cookie sheet that has been sprayed with a no-stick vegetable oil spray. Bake for 10 to 12 minutes in a preheated 350° oven.

If you like, sprinkle some grated low-fat mozzarella cheese over the crêpes before baking. Or top with a sauce. This recipe, made without the onions, celery, or chicken, would be a good choice for a simple sauce.

*If you're using canned broth, chill in the refrigerator first and remove any fat that rises to the top.

Each serving provides:			
193	Calories	18 g	Carbohydrate
16 g	Protein	337 mg	Sodium
6 g	Fat	32 mg	Cholesterol

Hawaiian Chicken Crêpes

See the recipe for Low-Fat Crêpes in this chapter, page 246.

Serves 4.

1	cup green onions, chopped
2	tablespoons safflower or canola oil
⅔	cup chicken stock
2	tablespoons flour
½	cup low-fat evaporated milk
1	can (14 oz.) pineapple chunks, drained (but reserve juice)
1	can (10 oz.) water chestnuts, drained
2	cups cooked chicken breast meat, diced
8	crêpes
	No-stick vegetable oil spray

In a skillet, sauté the green onions in the oil until tender. Combine the chicken stock and flour. Add to the skillet along with the milk. Stir over medium heat until thickened. Add the pineapple, water chestnuts, and chicken.

Fill the crêpes with 2 to 3 tablespoons of the filling. Roll up and place in a shallow baking dish (a cookie sheet is fine) that has been sprayed with the no-stick vegetable oil spray. Spoon the following sauce on top. Bake in a preheated 350° oven for 10 to 15 minutes, or until well heated through.

Sauce

1	tablespoon cornstarch
	Reserved pineapple juice

Dissolve the cornstarch in the pineapple juice. Cook, stirring constantly, until thickened and smooth. The amount of juice in canned fruit can vary. If the sauce is not thick enough, dissolve an additional 1 to 2 teaspoons of cornstarch in apple or orange juice, add to the sauce, and cook until it reaches the desired consistency.

Each serving provides:

513	Calories	62 g	Carbohydrate
34 g	Protein	209 mg	Sodium
14 g	Fat	69 mg	Cholesterol

10

Low-Fat Accompaniments, Pastry, Sauces, and Seasonings

We felt it was important to add this last chapter. There are no chicken recipes, but now that your dietary needs have changed, you might find invaluable those that are included here.

In addition, today's food budget seems to get stretched more and more every year. Having recipes on hand that are economical is becoming increasingly important. For instance, the zucchini pineapple recipe in this section costs only a fraction of the price of commercial canned pineapple, particularly if you grow your own zucchini, or if a friend or neighbor gives you some from their garden. Commercial no-salt seasonings are also considerably more expensive than homemade substitutes. And making your own yogurt is not only cost-cutting but very simple.

Coffee Can Bread

Use the 1-pound coffee cans with the plastic lids. This bread is not only cholesterol free, but also requires no kneading and is easier to make than a cake. Home baked bread can make a simple meal seem special. You can substitute 2 cups whole wheat flour for 2 cups of the white flour. You really should try this bread — we're addicted to it.

Serves 6.

1	package dry yeast
½	cup warm water
¼	teaspoon ginger
3	tablespoons sugar
13	oz. low-fat evaporated milk
1	teaspoon salt
2	tablespoons safflower or canola oil
4-4½	cups flour
	No-stick vegetable oil spray

In a large bowl combine the yeast, warm water, ginger, and 1 tablespoon of sugar. Let stand 15 minutes. Combine the evaporated milk, salt, oil, and 2 tablespoons of sugar. Stir until the sugar has dissolved, then add to the yeast mixture. Stir in the flour. Spray the inside of two coffee cans and their lids with the no-stick vegetable oil spray. Divide the dough in half and put into the cans. Cover with the plastic lids. Let stand until the lids pop — approximately 1½ hours. *Immediately* place the cans, uncovered, on the lowest rack of a preheated 350° oven and bake for 45 minutes. (We heat the oven just before the 1½ hours is up so it will be ready.)

Each serving provides:			
449	Calories	81 g	Carbohydrate
14 g	Protein	440 mg	Sodium
7 g	Fat	11 mg	Cholesterol

No-Fat Quick Whole Wheat Bread

Homemade bread in 1 hour and 5 minutes: 1 hour to bake, 5 minutes to assemble.

Serves 6.

2¼	cups whole wheat flour
1½	tablespoons sugar
1	teaspoon salt
2	teaspoons baking powder
¼	teaspoon baking soda
12	oz. freshly opened club soda (or beer)
2	teaspoons sesame seeds
	No-stick vegetable oil spray

Stir all of the ingredients together except the club soda and sesame seeds. Add the club soda and combine well. Empty the batter into a loaf pan that has been sprayed with the no-stick vegetable oil spray. Sprinkle the sesame seeds on top and bake in a preheated 350° oven for 1 hour.

Each serving provides:

171	Calories	36 g	Carbohydrate
6 g	Protein	558 mg	Sodium
0 g	Fat	0 mg	Cholesterol

Browned Flour*

This is a staple in many French Canadian homes. Passed down from grandmother to mother to daughter, you rarely see it in cookbooks, but all of the great cooks in Quebec know about it. It's particularly useful when preparing low-cholesterol dishes since it gives its own distinctive flavor to dishes that might otherwise suffer a bit because of the lack of salt and butter. The flour doesn't "lump" and it also gives a rich color to sauces and gravies.

A cast-iron frying pan is best for browning the flour. Place 2 cups of flour in a large, heavy-bottomed skillet. Stir the flour over low heat with a large cooking spoon. Keep stirring and scraping the bottom of the skillet so the flour does not stick. In a fairly short time the flour will begin to brown. Stir a little faster at this point so the flour does not burn. You want it a beige-brown color. Do not let it become too dark because it will get even darker when added to your sauces and gravies. Don't be tempted to turn the heat up if it seems to be slow in browning — once it gets started, it browns very quickly.

Store in a glass jar on kitchen shelf. It will last indefinitely. Use in place of any white flour called for in sauces or gravies.

*Nutritional analysis isn't possible.

Chili Oil

There's no question that dishes that are low in fat and salt can sometimes taste a little "flat." One trick to spice up a nourishing meal that's lacking in flavor is to add a small amount of sesame oil that's been heated with crushed red peppers. This can enliven many low-cholesterol dishes, particularly stir-fried vegetable dishes and many salad dressings. Experiment a bit and we're sure you'll come up with many taste delights.

Makes ½ cup.

½   cup Chinese sesame oil
⅓   cup crushed red peppers

Heat the sesame oil in a small saucepan until warm (not hot). Stir in the crushed red peppers. Let stand several hours, or overnight, at room temperature. Strain, pressing out all of the oil with the back of a spoon. Store in the refrigerator. Will keep indefinitely.

Each serving (1 tablespoon) provides:

123	Calories	0 g	Carbohydrate
0 g	Protein	0 mg	Sodium
14 g	Fat	0 mg	Cholesterol

Andrew's Low-Cholesterol Croutons*

If you don't have a spray bottle (a "mister"), by all means buy one. It's excellent for spraying oil onto a skillet for sautéing or for misting crumb-coated chicken for just a little added crunch. It's also a must for making these croutons. A large attractive jar filled with these and tied with a big red ribbon would be a welcome Christmas gift for a friend on a low-fat diet who loves salads.

1 slice bread yields 1 cup croutons

1	slice bread
½	teaspoon garlic powder
½	teaspoon Parmesan cheese

Place the bread on a cookie sheet and mist lightly with water. Sprinkle with the garlic powder and Parmesan cheese on both sides. Bake in a preheated 300° oven for 12 minutes. Turn the bread over and bake an additional 10 minutes. Remove from the oven and *immediately* cut into cubes.

*Nutritional analysis isn't possible.

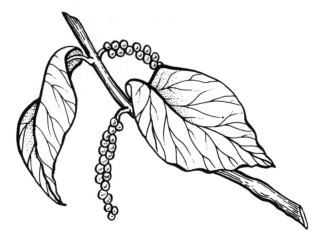

Great Low-Cholesterol Pastry

This pastry dough is wonderfully easy to handle. Unlike some pastry, it rolls out beautifully regardless of how much you handle it. We like it best made with pastry flour, but all-purpose flour works well also.

Makes enough pastry for 2 double crusts plus 1 single crust.

½	cup low-fat milk
¼	cup white vinegar
1	pound soft margarine
4	cups flour
¼	cup wheat germ

Combine the milk and vinegar and set aside. Cut the margarine into the flour until it has the consistency of corn meal, using either a pastry cutter or your fingers, or both. Stir in the wheat germ. Add the milk and vinegar mixture all at once. Form a ball and wrap in plastic wrap. Store in the refrigerator until needed. It will keep for 2 to 3 weeks.

This pastry should be chilled for at least 2 hours before rolling out. Make sure you roll on a well-floured board or counter.

To bake a single crust without shrinkage, prick the pastry with a fork, chill for 15 minutes, and line the uncooked pie shell with foil and fill with pie weights or raw beans before baking. Bake in a preheated 450° oven for 10 minutes.

Each crust provides:			
1,048	Calories	81 g	Carbohydrate
14 g	Protein	994 mg	Sodium
75 g	Fat	1 mg	Cholesterol

Perfect Pastry for a Single Crust

This pastry is difficult to roll out, although it can be done between two pieces of plastic wrap. It works best when "patted" into a pie plate.

Makes 1 single pie crust.

1½   cups all-purpose flour
1½   teaspoons sugar
¼   teaspoon salt'
⅓   cup plus 1 tablespoon canola oil
2   tablespoons low-fat milk or lemon juice

Mix the flour, sugar, and salt in a 9-inch pie plate. Stir together the oil and milk (or lemon juice). Pour into the flour mixture. Stir with a fork until the liquid has been absorbed by the flour mixture. Use your fingers to press the dough over the bottom and up the sides of the pan. Flute the edges. Prick the bottom with a fork. Bake in a preheated 400° oven for 10 to 12 minutes, or until golden brown.

Note: The pie shell can be lined with foil and filled with pie weights or uncooked beans to help prevent shrinkage.

Each pie crust provides:

1,482	Calories	151 g	Carbohydrate
20 g	Protein	559 mg	Sodium
88 g	Fat	1 mg	Cholesterol

Spiced Prunes

A friend of ours first made these intending to use them as a garnish for game dinners. One evening, though, she was caught short with nothing to serve with drinks and decided to serve these as an hors d'oeuvre. They were so popular she has been serving them as appetizers ever since. We find them a great accompaniment to many chicken dishes. It's nice to have a dual-purpose item on your shelf!

Serves 12.

1	pound dried, pitted prunes
2	cups brown sugar
2½	cups malt vinegar
1¼	cups water
3	small sticks cinnamon
¾	teaspoon mace
¾	teaspoon whole cloves

Combine all of the above ingredients in a large saucepan. Let sit for 1 hour. Transfer the saucepan to the stove and simmer the prunes gently for 15 to 20 minutes. Pack into hot sterilized jars and seal. If you're going to use them frequently, it's not necessary to seal them, but they must be stored in the refrigerator. (These prunes will keep one month in the refrigerator.) Makes 4 cups.

Each serving provides:

237	Calories	63 g	Carbohydrate
1 g	Protein	14 mg	Sodium
0 g	Fat	0 mg	Cholesterol

Zucchini Pineapple

An amazing recipe — the zucchini actually tastes like canned pineapple. We don't know where or when the recipe originated, but we still get requests for it every summer.

Makes about 16 pints.

1	gallon peeled and seeded zucchini, cut into cubes
2½-	
3½	cups sugar
1	large can (48 oz.) pineapple juice
¼	teaspoon yellow food coloring
2	teaspoons pineapple extract*
1½	cups lemon juice

Place all of the above ingredients in a large preserving kettle or Dutch oven and bring to a boil. Reduce heat and simmer for 20 minutes. Pack in sterile jars and process in a boiling water bath for 20 minutes.

*If you can't find the pineapple extract, your zucchini pineapple will still taste great.

Each serving (¼ cup) provides:

27	Calories	7 g	Carbohydrate
0 g	Protein	1 mg	Sodium
0 g	Fat	0 mg	Cholesterol

Mexican Tomato Salsa (Uncooked)

Because this isn't cooked, it has a lovely fresh flavor.

Makes approximately 2 cups.

3 large tomatoes, peeled, seeded, and drained
4 large green onions, including tops
1 can (4 oz.) whole green chilies, drained and seeded
1 tablespoon jalapeño peppers, chopped
1 tablespoon olive oil
1 tablespoon red wine vinegar
1 teaspoon salt or no-salt seasoning
2 tablespoons fresh cilantro leaves, chopped

Finely chop the tomatoes, green onions, chilies, and jalapeño peppers and combine in a medium-sized mixing bowl. Add the olive oil, vinegar, and salt and stir to blend the ingredients. Let stand at least 30 minutes. Add the chopped cilantro at serving time.

The salsa may be made 4 hours in advance, kept covered, and chilled. Bring to room temperature before serving.

Each serving (2 tablespoons) provides:			
16	Calories	2 g	Carbohydrate
0 g	Protein	183 mg	Sodium
1 g	Fat	0 mg	Cholesterol

Mexican Tomato Salsa (Cooked)

Makes 6 cups.

2	large cans (28 oz. each) tomatoes
½	cup onion, chopped
1	sweet red pepper, seeded and chopped
1	can (4 oz.) green chilies, drained, seeded, and chopped
1	tablespoon jalapeño pepper, finely chopped
1	can (5½ oz.) tomato paste
3	cloves garlic, minced
½	cup red wine vinegar
3	tablespoons lime juice (bottled is fine)
2	tablespoons sugar
1	tablespoon chili powder
1	teaspoon salt or no-salt seasoning
1	teaspoon oregano
½	teaspoon Tabasco sauce
2	tablespoons fresh cilantro leaves, chopped

Combine all of the ingredients, except the cilantro, in a Dutch oven and bring to a boil over high heat, stirring constantly (break up the tomatoes with a fork). When it reaches a full rolling boil, reduce heat to medium and cook, stirring frequently, until the salsa has thickened (about 30 to 35 minutes). Stir in the cilantro and seal in hot, sterilized jars. (Or store unsealed in the refrigerator for up to one month.)

Each serving (2 tablespoons) provides:

14	Calories	3 g	Carbohydrate
1 g	Protein	142 mg	Sodium
0 g	Fat	0 mg	Cholesterol

No-Salt Seasoning

You'll notice many recipes calling for no-salt seasoning throughout this book. Commercial brands are available, but it's a simple matter to make your own. The following is the one we've used in testing the recipes for this book. Use it whenever you want to add a nice "salty" taste to soups, stews, sauces, gravies, etc. Make extra and give some to a friend on a salt-restricted diet. We find it to be preferable to any over-the-counter brands we've tried.

Makes 1 cup.

4   tablespoons dry mustard
4   tablespoons onion powder
2   tablespoons white pepper
1   tablespoon plus 1 teaspoon garlic powder
2   tablespoons paprika
2   tablespoons thyme (ground or powdered)
1   teaspoon basil (ground or powdered)

Stir all of the above ingredients together until well mixed. Store in a glass jar and use as needed. This keeps indefinitely.

Each serving (1 teaspoon) provides:			
7	Calories	1 g	Carbohydrate
0 g	Protein	1 mg	Sodium
0 g	Fat	0 mg	Cholesterol

Low-Fat Cream Sau

Don't worry about the sauce tasting of evaporat
use the lemon pepper. If you don't have any lemo
only for this recipe, but also for many others in t
it's a low-salt brand.)

2	tablespoons soft margarine
2	tablespoons flour
1	teaspoon chicken bouillon mix
1	cup low-fat evaporated milk
½	teaspoon no-salt seasoning or salt
½	teaspoon lemon pepper
	Pinch of paprika

Melt the margarine in a small saucepan. Stir in the flour and bouillon mix. Gradually stir in the evaporated milk and seasonings. Cook over medium heat, stirring constantly, until the sauce thickens (about 3 to 5 minutes).

Each serving (1 tablespoon) provides:

29	Calories	3 g	Carbohydrate
1 g	Protein	123 mg	Sodium
1 g	Fat	1 mg	Cholesterol

Low-Fat Cream Sauce 2

Makes 1¼ cups.

3   tablespoons skim milk powder
1   tablespoon cornstarch
½   teaspoon chicken bouillon mix
1   cup skim milk
1   tablespoon soft margarine

Place all of the ingredients in a small saucepan and stir with a wire whisk over medium heat until the mixture comes to a boil and thickens (about 3 minutes).

Each serving (1 tablespoon) provides:			
17	Calories	2 g	Carbohydrate
1 g	Protein	52 mg	Sodium
1 g	Fat	0 mg	Cholesterol

"Sun-Dried" Tomatoes Made in the Oven*

Sun-dried tomatoes can really dress up many otherwise bland dishes. Many supermarkets carry sun-dried tomatoes now, but if you live in an area where they're not readily available, try the following method.

Cut ¼ inch off the stem end of ripe tomatoes. Slice into ¼-inch slices lengthwise, but don't cut all the way through. The tomatoes should end up shaped like a fan. Lay open on a rack placed on a cookie sheet. Salt the cut surface. Bake in a preheated 200° oven for 8 hours. Or place in the oven for 6 hours, turn the oven off, and leave in overnight; in the morning, turn on the oven to 200° and bake for an additional hour. The tomatoes should be pliable, not brittle. Place in jars and cover with olive oil. Add one or two cloves of garlic to each jar. These keep one to two months in the refrigerator.

*Nutritional analysis isn't possible.

Homemade Yogurt

Yogurt is used in many recipes in this book — it will come to be a staple item in your refrigerator. Homemade yogurt is especially delicious. This recipe couldn't be easier and is economical as well.

Makes 2 quarts.

6   cups low-fat milk
6   tablespoons skim milk powder
2   tablespoons low-fat yogurt

Combine the milk and milk powder in a saucepan and bring to almost boiling. Let cool to lukewarm. Add the yogurt. Stir well and put into oven-proof glass jars. Let sit, uncovered, in a warm oven overnight. To warm the oven, simply turn the indicator to the warm setting and when the light goes off, turn the oven off. Place the jars in the oven as soon as the light goes off.

Each serving (2 tablespoons) provides:			
13	Calories	1 g	Carbohydrate
1 g	Protein	14 mg	Sodium
0 g	Fat	2 mg	Cholesterol

Yogurt "Cheese"

Makes ¾ cup.

Place 1 cup of yogurt in a deep strainer that's been lined with a double thickness of cheesecloth. Place the strainer over a bowl (to catch the whey that drains out), and let sit in the refrigerator for at least 24 hours. Remove from the strainer. You now have a low-fat product that makes a good base for dips, sauces, and dressings. Keeps one week in the refrigerator.

Each serving (2 tablespoons) provides:			
25	Calories	1 g	Carbohydrate
3 g	Protein	18 mg	Sodium
1 g	Fat	1 mg	Cholesterol

Yogurt Mayonnaise

Makes 1 cup.

½   cup yogurt cheese (see p. 268)
½   cup low-fat ricotta cheese
1   tablespoon fresh lemon juice
½   teaspoon Dijon mustard
⅛   teaspoon Worcestershire sauce
     Freshly ground black pepper to taste

   Whisk all of the above ingredients together. This will keep in the refrigerator for up to one week.

Each serving (1 tablespoon) provides:			
12	Calories	1 g	Carbohydrate
2 g	Protein	16 mg	Sodium
0 g	Fat	1 mg	Cholesterol

Cumberland Sauce

Wonderful with poultry or game.

Makes 1½ cups.

1   tablespoon cornstarch
1   cup port wine
1   **cup red currant jelly**
1   teaspoon prepared mustard
¼   teaspoon grated orange rind

Mix the cornstarch and wine in a saucepan. Add the remaining ingredients. Bring to a boil. Reduce heat and simmer slowly until clear. Serve immediately, or store in the refrigerator and reheat before serving.

Each serving (2 tablespoons) provides:

102	Calories	21 g	Carbohydrate
0 g	Protein	12 mg	Sodium
0 g	Fat	0 mg	Cholesterol

Index

About the Authors

Eleanor Clark is a food consultant for a large chain of super-markets, a newspaper food columnist, and a registered nurse. She also has a bi-weekly cooking show on Canadian television. Co-author of *The Absolute Beginner's Cookbook*, Eleanor is married and the mother of four grown children.

Jackie Eddy is a newspaper food editor and cookbook author (*Slicing, Hooking, and Cooking, Starters and Bits*, and *The Second Slice*). Co-author of *The Absolute Beginner's Cookbook*, she has demonstrated recipes from her books on Canadian television. Jackie is also married and the mother of four grown children.

During the authors' first project together, *The Absolute Beginner's Cookbook*, they discovered they made a great team. *Low-Fat Gourmet Chicken* is their second joint project. Developing over 200 tasty and interesting recipes for skinless chicken was indeed a challenge. With the enthuiastic assistance of family, friends, and fellow professionals, all of whom made themselves available for the many Sunday night recipe tastings, this book became a reality.